Painting Western Character Studies

Cowboy with a Rifle. Oil on panel, 21″ x 28″ (53.34 x 71.12 cm). Private collection.

Painting Western Character Studies

Techniques in Oil

BY JOSEPH DAWLEY
AS TOLD TO GLORIA DAWLEY AND ROBERT KOLBE

WATSON-GUPTILL PUBLICATIONS/NEW YORK

Library of Congress Cataloging in Publication Data
Dawley, Joseph.
   Painting western character studies.
   Includes index.
   1.Indians of North America — Pictorial works.
2.Cowboys in art.   3. Painting — Technique.   I. Dawley,
Gloria.   II. Kolbe, Robert, 1931–   III. Title.
ND1302.D37 1975   751.4′5   75-17889
ISBN 0-8230-3877-7

First Printing, 1975

Edited by Susan Davis
Designed by James Craig and Bob Fillie
Set in 12 point Memphis by Gerard Associates/Graphics Art, Inc.
Printed by Parish Press, Inc., New York
Bound by A. Horowitz and Son, New York

I dedicate this book to the many people
who not only willingly posed,
but provided necessary background information
to assure the accuracy of this book.

Acknowledgments

I wish to gratefully acknowledge the help, patience, and understanding unfailingly provided by Robert Kolbe, our staff, our children, and Watson-Guptill, without which this book could never have been successfully completed.

Contents

Introduction

Indian Girl. Sepia on board, 15″ x 15½″ (38.1 x 39.37 cm). This very young and pretty Indian maiden, whom I painted in a loose monotone of raw umber and white, has a more artistic feeling because of "brushiness." The loose quality does not mean, however, that I have not taken pains to approach this in a realistic manner and to do the features carefully. Note the variety of brushstrokes that I used. Collection Robert Schermerhorn.

This book combines elements of my last two books — getting personality and character down on Masonite or canvas and painting problem materials. But its real intent is to take a 1970s look at a part of our culture I know well — Western characters, Indian and white, men and women.

I'm familiar with this section of America because I was born there and lived there until I was 25. When I was growing up, I was fortunate enough to travel over some of the Southwest with my late Dad, a partner in an ice and cold-storage company. He had to make the rounds of the plants as part of his job, and I often went with him. I saw the desolation of West Texas, Arkansas, and Oklahoma towns and nearby Indian reservations before I was 10. I'll never forget them.

Now when I go back there, I visit ranches of men my father knew and the adjoining Indian settlements. The West has a personality all its own, and after living in the East now for fourteen years, I can look back on it with, I believe, a better perspective than if I had never left.

As a grownup I've more feeling for the West than I had as a youngster. I see people's problems as a boy can't see them. But it's still those old memories that provide the clues to understanding today's West.

So I've tried to put together a book that's about people who are trying hard to cling to traditional ways. In talking to them and painting them, I think I've also improved my insight into what makes a good character painting.

I believe the techniques and approaches in this book can help other artists, as much as they've helped me, come to some understanding of painting character studies. With them we should be better able to paint personalities in the West — or anywhere we choose.

Pueblo with Long Hair. Oil on panel, 10" x 11" (25.4 x 27.94 cm). I feel this young Pueblo man is a fine representation of young Indian manhood. Note the strength and directness of the eyes and mouth. The loose, brushy painting technique I've used, together with the flowing hair, illustrate the free spirit very much enjoyed by this group of people. Private collection.

Materials and Methods

My preferences in materials, colors, and painting methods keep evolving — and for the better, I believe. In describing what I work with, I've tried to cover changes I've adopted recently and explain the reasons for these switches.

Painting is a combination of thought process and execution. The Old Masters prove it. They were great researchers in paint. Perhaps the greatest problem with fine painting today is that their knowledge was not passed on, and worse, painters and public seem unconcerned about the seriousness of this loss. Therefore we must rediscover their techniques one by one.

Studying materials and application is an exciting quest toward recovering knowledge of the Old Masters and with it producing a new renaissance in painting.

Color Palette

Here are the paints I'm likely to use in full-color pictures, along with an evaluation of their qualities:

ALIZARIN CRIMSON. Cool, transparent red used sparingly for skin tones. A bit less delicate than genuine rose madder.

BURNT SIENNA. A must. This red-brown mixes well with other colors, is great for skin tones, and is a good drier.

BURNT UMBER. I use this warm brown sparingly for glazing.

CADMIUM ORANGE. Bright, opaque color that I use solely for painting an orange.

CADMIUM RED. This bright, opaque red comes in a variety of shades and is good for skin tones. I use the light, medium, and deepest shades quite often.

CADMIUM YELLOW. Another bright, opaque color in a variety of shades, which is very useful for reproducing gold or candlelight. Mixed with black or blue, it can also be used for a bright green. When mixed with raw umber, it becomes a muted green.

CERULEAN BLUE. Opaque, sky blue, which is appropriate for pottery.

COBALT BLUE. A bright, but more transparent blue, which mixes well with other colors.

COBALT VIOLET. A clear, bright violet or purple for giving paintings a spot of color or for shadows in the fold of a drape.

COBALT YELLOW (aureolin). Another must. This bright, transparent hue dries quickly and is excellent for glazes. Sometimes I mix it with cadmium red deep for skin tone glazes.

GOLD OCHRE (transparent). Excellent for thin glazes, especially in skin tones — particularly for the American Indian.

INDIAN RED. I used it sparingly when I paint people. Maybe one out of every ten or twelve character studies has any of this color at all.

But it's great for clothing — if you don't want the red to be overpowering.

IVORY BLACK. A cool black, great for everything, even skin tones. Never paint another color over pure ivory black or lamp black for cracking may occur.

LAMP BLACK. Warmer than ivory black and can be used for anything. Mixed with Mars yellow (or yellow ochre) and burnt sienna, it makes a beautiful brown, depending on how well you use it.

MARS YELLOW. Muted yellow substitute for yellow ochre. Fair for skin tones, but seldom as effective as yellow ochre.

OXIDE OF CHROMIUM. A beautiful, opaque, pastel green. Complements every color it's used with.

PHTHALOCYANINE BLUE. Extremely strong, transparent, slightly greenish blue. Use very little because of its great strength. For example, 40 parts white to one part phthalo blue produces the sky on a clear day.

RAW SIENNA. Earthy yellow, darker than yellow ochre. Good for skin tone and wood, tinting and glazing.

RAW UMBER. Very soft, warm, neutral brown. Makes a good, blackish glazing color mixed with ultramarine blue. I also like Winsor & Newton's more greenish, cool raw umber that I mix with white and a tiny bit of ultramarine blue for a gray. I also use this raw umber for skin tones.

ULTRAMARINE BLUE. A lovely, semitransparent blue, it mixes well with other colors. When mixed with raw umber, it's good for tinting or wet-in-wet painting.

VENETIAN RED. Much brighter than burnt sienna, this earth red is one of my favorite colors for skin tones and many other things. It mixes well with other colors and is good for underpainting, overpainting, and glazing.

VIRIDIAN GREEN. A transparent emerald color that's fine for glazing. Mixed with yellows, it makes bright greens. Mixed with raw umber, it produces a more somber color.

YELLOW OCHRE. An earth yellow, good for skin tones and gold objects and for mixing with other colors to make shades of browns, greens, and somber oranges.

The Whites

The most important thing in this book may be what I have to say about the two white paints I use — flake white and underpainting white. This is because the basis of oil painting is mixing white with color to make tones, as well as transitional grays — the secret of the Old Masters oil technique.

FLAKE WHITE. A basic lead carbonate and a good all-around white. It's great for priming canvas and panels and good for underpainting because of its elasticity.

But here's a very big caution. Flake white should always be pure lead white, which is becoming less and less easy to buy. There is only one brand I consider true flake white. Manufactured by Utrecht Linens, in Boston, Mass., it's basic lead white with linseed oil. Winsor & Newton also makes a flake white that's a lead white—their Cremnitz white, ground with poppy oil. But I can't guarantee how well it will work for underpainting and scumbling because of the poppy oil. I use it only for finishing touches.

Most other paint manufacturers around the world are adding zinc to lead white. This absolutely ruins painting. Achieving traditional Old Masters style is impossible for me with a zinc white because it takes on an entirely different consistency and dries much more slowly. Also it seems impossible to achieve translucence with zinc white. What's the result? Centuries-long Old Masters durability is lost, and tinting and scumbling are impossible. You can't tint or scumble with titanium whites because they take weeks and weeks to dry and don't have the right consistency.

Why are the big paint companies doing this to lead white? It's hard to say. Could be, it's easier or less expensive to make. The problem is they're manufacturing paint for amateurs—there must be 92 amateurs for every professional in the field. And the solid craftsman is being left out.

Some will complain that basic lead-based flake white yellows and ages a shade darker. But it doesn't look bad. In fact, it really seems to improve the appearance of almost all paintings. Most artists tend toward the red side of the palette, and flake white—yellowing as it does—sometimes actually makes a painting look better! If there's an overwhelming need in a specific situation for something not to yellow, use underpainting white instead, and paint over it with a little titanium white if you feel the need.

UNDERPAINTING WHITE. This is a thick and pasty titanium white. It's quick drying and good for scumbling. I use Winsor & Newton for the simple reason that they guarantee it. Grumbacher's M.O. white may be good, but it's not guaranteed.

Monotone Palette

Demonstrations 1–22 are monotone oil exercises that appear in black and white, although I actually do them in raw umber, white, and sometimes ultramarine blue. I always put more paint than needed on the palette so I don't have to slow down to mix more. I may have to throw away a little paint, but it's well worth it.

I lay out a five-tone range. Tone #0 is pure white. Tone #1 is about 95 percent white and 5 percent raw umber. Tone #2 is about 90 percent white and 10 percent raw umber. Tone #3 is about 75 percent white and 25 percent raw umber. Tone #4 is pure raw umber from the tube. Pure ultramarine blue and raw umber make a darker black than tone #4. I refer to all these tones by their numbers in the steps in each demonstration.

Not watching which raw umber you use can lead to a bit of confusion as various brands differ in their covering power. You'll have to use twice as much raw umber as indicated above to produce the needed tones with some brands. Percentages are only approximations. You'll have to experiment to match tones. When I add ultramarine blue to the raw umber in laying out these tones, I also change the percentages a bit.

Skin Tone Palette

Because there are six demonstrations in this book in color, I'll review my skin tone palette. It consists of white, Venetian red, yellow ochre, raw umber, raw sienna, and ultramarine blue. Raw umber and ultramarine blue are mixed for a black. As the painting develops, I add burnt sienna and white, as well as an ivory black–and–white gray. I used to use a cool highlight of white, yellow ochre, and ivory black, but I've dropped ivory black from my principal highlight mixture. Now I get along with a combination of yellow ochre and white, which produces a warm highlight, rather than the cool highlight I preferred in the earlier books.

Painting Medium

I've switched from damar varnish medium to copal resin medium because it's harder. Talking to Frederick Taubes and reading his work have convinced me that he's right. I prefer Taubes' copal painting medium, both light and heavy. I usually use the heavy. Then I follow with copal concentrate, which is a very thick mixture of copal resin and stand oil. It's excellent, but should be reserved for the final stages of a painting because it's tough to paint over.

I may use turpentine to thin paint when I'm working on the beginning steps of the monotone palette. Later I use the paints with painting medium. When I begin overpainting, I simply add more medium. When the painting is completely dry, I paint medium over the entire surface and then use it along with the

#1 #2 #3 #4

Monotone Palette. Here's the palette that I use for Demonstrations 1–22. Tone #0, not shown here, is pure white. Tones #1, #2, and #3 are mixtures of white and increasing percentages of raw umber. Tone #4 is pure raw umber.

paints. When I do heavy reworking of an area, I use even heavier painting medium.

Varnish

Grumbacher damar retouch varnish is the best temporary varnish to spray on a painting when it's completely dry.

After a picture is at least one year old, the best way to do a final varnish is to give the painting one coat of Taubes copal varnish with a nice soft brush. When it's dry, put it back in the frame and hang it on the wall again for two months. Then take it out of the frame and finish up with a coat of damar varnish. This way you'll have hard resin on the bottom, protected by soft resin on top. As it ages, you can clean the painting by carefully removing the soft resin on top. The copal resin underneath will be hard enough not to come up during this operation, and the paint will be left unscathed. This is Frederick Taubes' way of doing it, and I think it's the best.

Brushes

I use several types of sable and bristle brushes for the many effects in my paintings.

SABLE. For smooth, delicate strokes, I use flat, soft, short-haired brushes in widths from ⅛" to 1", as well as a #2 or #3 sable watercolor brush, which points well for detail work. I bypass long-haired sables designed for detail oil work. They aren't good quality. Sometimes I use a fan sable for blending.

BRISTLE. These I reserve for rougher effects of textured materials. Natural-curve white bristle brushes are my preference in sizes from ⅜" to ¾". For smaller work, I switch to sable.

Cleaning Brushes

Artist's turpentine is an unnecessary expense. A good grade of gum turpentine, if it isn't yellowed, is just as good.

I fill two jars with turpentine for cleaning brushes. One is for rinsing to remove excess paint. The other is for the final soaking and cleaning. I make sure to wipe brushes carefully to remove all paint. Then I place them bristles up in a large-mouthed jar that I keep close at hand.

I use anything soft for rags. Socks, sheets, even underwear will do if they are torn into pieces about 18" (45 cm) square. Don't con-tinue to use a dirty rag for wiping brushes. Throw it out and use a clean one.

Palette and Knives

I use 12" × 16" (30.48 × 40.64 cm) paper tear-away palettes without thumb holes. I prefer not to hold the palette because I usually have three going at the same time for most paintings. One is for skin tones, another for background, and the third for painting clothing and props.

I use a palette knife only for mixing colors. So any palette knife that's handy is okay.

Painting Surfaces

Masonite and linen are my preferences. Here are their qualities:

MASONITE. Easy to work on, it has long life and is more damage resistant than linen. It can easily be cut to fit the design of the painting. I use ⅛" untempered boards that come in 4' × 8' (121.92 × 243.84 cm) sheets, which I cut into thirds for storing.

Two thin coats of gesso go over the rough side of the Masonite, and I let it dry for six weeks in the warmest, driest place available. Then I sometimes put Winsor & Newton oil painting primer over the smooth surface with a clean cloth, leaving a very thin coating. This should be left to dry for at least six weeks.

Underpainting white may be applied to the board instead of oil painting primer. Generally, however, I simply stop with the gesso. I think underpainting white may be painted under or over flake white without cracking occurring if you use cobalt painting medium in your paint.

CANVAS. For a large picture I may use stretched canvas instead of Masonite. The rougher surface of the canvas helps produce a brushy look, which helps a bigger work. I do all the stretching and preparing myself, using smooth- or medium-texture, top-grade Belgium linen.

Joining the stretcher strips together, I square the corners and place the frame on top of the linen before cutting it, making sure to leave very ample overlaps. Wrapping the canvas around the frame, I secure it on one long side by a tack in the middle of the overlap. I use #8 blued cut tacks with large heads. Tacking again on the opposite side, I pull the linen fairly taut with canvas pliers. Securing the short sides in the same way, I work around the frame, stretching the linen tightly as I tack. Corners are folded and tacked for neatness.

I prepare rabbit-skin glue according to package directions. Applied to the surface of the linen with a sponge, it shrinks and tightens the canvas, giving it extra firmness. When it's completely dry, I lightly sand the surface and apply a second coat. To seal off the back, I sometimes brush on a 5 to 6 percent formaldehyde solution. Most of the time I do nothing.

When the canvas has dried sufficiently, I give it a coat of Winsor & Newton oil painting primer and let it sit for at least eight weeks. I used to use a different method—rubbing flake white into the surface with a turpentine-soaked cloth. When this was dry, I applied a second coat of flake white with a brush. This is still a good method. I just decided to use the other one.

Painting Techniques

Here are the painting techniques I use throughout the book:

ALLA PRIMA. Painting wet paint on a field of wet paint is a basic method of applying paint. Pictures can be done completely by this method with no overpainting or underpainting. When the paint is applied thickly, it's called "impasto."

GLAZING. After the underpainting dries, the glaze—a transparent layer of color usually thinned with painting medium—can be applied. I spread painting medium over all the dry paint, dip a soft sable into the medium, and then into transparent or semitransparent color. Brushing it over the area produces the bright, transparent effect of glazing.

TINTING. This process is similar to glazing. A thin layer of opaque color is used to modify an underlying layer of dry color. But the tint is thin enough to let the underpainting show through faintly. For example, this can be done with skin tones painted with a mixture of flake white, yellow ochre, and Venetian red. I take painting medium and thin a mixture of burnt sienna and white to apply lightly over the dried skin tone passage to produce a tint.

BRUSHY. The effect produced by the visible, flowing brushstrokes that I often use to show texture.

UNDERPAINTING. This is the first coat (or coats) of paint meant to be improved with layers of paint added after it has dried. For example, raw umber and white as preliminary indication of lights and darks constitute the underpainting. When they are later painted over with ivory black and raw sienna, that is overpainting.

OVERPAINTING. This is a glaze, tint, or scumble that completely covers the underpainting.

SCUMBLING. Paint is dragged over a partially dry surface. This can be done as an impasto or as a glaze or tint. I use a soft sable brush, never allowing it to dip into the underlying color or loosen the lower layers. A unique effect is produced as the scumbled color partially mixes with, partially rides on top of, the underlying color.

Since there is so much disagreement on paint, painting medium, varnishes, etc., I can only use experience and common sense as a guide. All my views are my own and remain unprejudiced. As for the longevity of a painting, however, it is my opinion that you should learn to paint a good picture first, then worry about how long it will last.

Bandana

Pueblo. Oil on canvas, 16" x 20" (40.64 x 50.8 cm). This Indian study has many prominent aspects, among which are the depth of the man's expression, the neckware, and the bandana. Obviously, a bandana can be used in many ways, and this study illustrates an entirely different manner than the one in the demonstration. Notice the indication of a fabric pattern as well as the rendering of the elaborate bow on the side of the head. Private collection.

Bandanas give cowboys their brightest touch of color. These large, vivid kerchiefs, usually with a white design on a brilliant red background, are multipurpose. Worn around the throat, they protect riders from dust created by moving horses and cattle. When the range is particularly dry, cowboys pull bandanas up to cover nose and mouth. If the weather is hot, they use bandanas to mop their brows. Or they may wet bandanas and wear them around their necks, faces, or foreheads to help keep cool.

A bandana can also be used as a marker or signal. By tying his kerchief to a post, the cowboy shows others which canyon to explore for strays. Waving it as a bright red flag, he can attract attention across wide stretches of flat terrain.

A bandana can be used as a carrying sack. You can stuff a surprising amount of duffle into these huge handkerchiefs. Tying the four corners together makes a compact carrying bag like the ones hobos and tramps used in the Depression to tote their belongings on the end of a broomstick.

Finally, a bandana over a pile of straw or grass makes a nice pillow.

To have it handy for whatever use, the cowboy at work usually wears a bandana. So if we omit the gay neckwear when we paint him on the range, we miss an opportunity for authenticity and color.

In painting this bandana, I did the rendering and following stages as casually as possible. I wanted to make sure I achieved softness and complete lack of rigidity. I was aiming for a kind of vagueness in the bandana's folds and knot. I applied two glazes and waited three times for stickiness or complete drying. Wrinkles and shadows were done initially by varying the consistency of raw umber with painting medium.

While most names for cowboy gear are of Spanish origin, it's interesting that the word "bandana" is from the Hindu and refers to its method of dyeing.

Step 1. This subject will probably be one of, if not the, simplest to render in this book. Not only does the nature of the subject make this true, but the fact that so much of it is hidden by the shirt and hair of today's cowboy.

I begin by blocking in the front portion of the bandana, the knot, and the kerchief ends with a raw umber glaze, indicating a couple of wrinkles with less highly thinned raw umber. After completing this, I allow this step to become sticky.

Step 2. In this step I'm only using one process: I'm blending white into the existing raw umber drawing completed in Step 1. Since the surface paint into which I'm working is sticky, I'm able to do this without destroying the underlying wrinkles and dark areas in the knot. The raw umber and white blend together as I work, creating the lights, darks, and in-between tones indicated in Step 1. I now allow this step to become sticky before beginning Step 3.

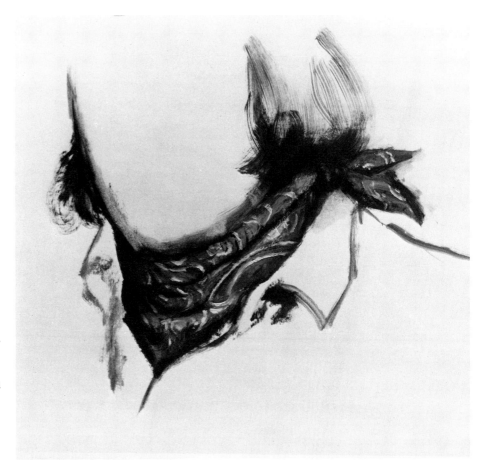

Step 3. I brush white into the light areas of the folds and kerchief ends, which really is the entire kerchief area except for the shadow areas. This lays the groundwork for the design, which I will paint in next. I brush on the predominantly white design, but for the few dark lines in the pattern I use raw umber. This step dries completely before I continue.

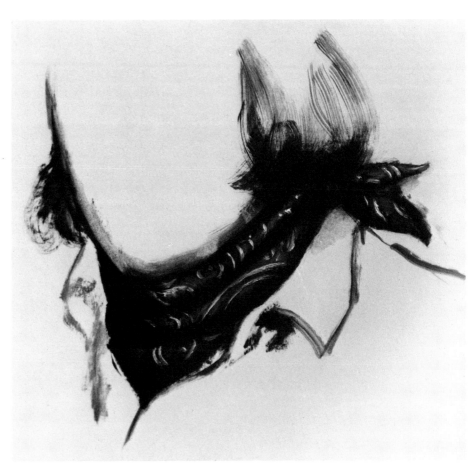

Step 4. With heavy painting medium and raw umber, I glaze over the entire kerchief, including the design. This, of course, darkens the design, but the mixture is applied thinly enough to still allow the pattern to show through. Then, over the lighter portions of the bandana, such as the ends and the tops of the folds, I glaze flake white and heavy painting medium. I go over the design as well, but not thickly enough to obliterate it. I blend this with a soft sable brush into the raw umber glaze to create the roundness of the folds. The final thing is to reemphasize the design, for which I use flake white and copal concentrate.

Feather

Raindancer with a Spear.
Oil on panel, 16" x 24" (40.64 x 60.96 cm). Here is an interesting combination of two different uses of feathers frequently found in the Indian costume. The headdress is a very loose collection of feathers more or less gathered together at random. The feathered decoration flowing down his back is very fluffy in contrast and highly organized. Both require different techniques discussed in Demonstrations 2 and 11 as well as at various other points within this book. Private collection.

Feathers, like most Indian apparel and decoration, are taken straight from nature and are extremely expressive of the Indian way of life, so close to the heartbeat of existence. More than other ornaments, feathers show clearly the Indian's life of freedom. The consistent use of plumage shows respect for the soaring creatures of the outdoors. Indians so love birds that many took names from the most brave and defiant of them. Feathers are still used today in tribal costumes, but gone are many of the birds that once produced varied adornment. Their fate was linked to that of the Plains Indians themselves. Vanished forever is the passenger pigeon, once numerous enough to darken skies at midday. Almost gone is the magnificent bald eagle. And hawks, rooks, and blackbirds are much depleted.

Painting a feather requires some of the light touch of the airy subject. So, until well into the painting, I'll use a thin, delicate approach and more painting medium than usual. In addition to the four tones of raw umber and white used in most of the demonstrations, I create a cool brown of raw umber and ultramarine blue. I control its darkness with painting medium. When designing the feather, an inverted V at the tip will help it look more natural. Feathers commonly part at one such place or another. To develop a "feather-like" appearance, I apply a glaze over the rendering of pinfeathers and the center vein. This glaze is critically important because as soon as it's sticky, I introduce flake white and use it with the original color to blend and scumble the pinfeathers.

I think you'll find that feathers are not only fun to paint, but the single item of adornment that, if well done, will give the most authentic and colorful air to Indian paintings.

Step 1. For this demonstration I'm not using my usual five tones. Instead, I've mixed approximately three parts raw umber and one part ultramarine blue together, creating a cool brown color. This particular color is very helpful either as an underpainting color for feathers, or as in this case, the primary color used to render a feather. In fact, it is the only color on my palette for this demonstration until Step 4, when I'll add flake white. The color's darkness is increased or decreased depending on the amount of painting medium mixed with it.

I begin by doing a line or contour drawing of the feather. The whole feather, including the center vein, is rendered with a flat sable brush. A lot of painting medium is mixed with a little bit of the basic color to indicate the dark tip.

Step 2. In this step my basic aim is to achieve a "featherlike" appearance. To do this, I first darken the center vein. Next, I mix the paint with a lot of painting medium and indicate a few of the pinfeathers radiating diagonally from the center vein. Also, I darken the tip, still using a lot of painting medium, and give the right-hand outer edge more of a feathery look by making it a bit more jagged.

Step 3. To render the dark tip, I use the basic color with very little painting medium mixed in. I lightly glaze over the remaining pinfeather area. I do this very thinly to allow the previous indications of pinfeathers to show through. At the same time I leave some of the white background exposed to create the whitish areas of the feather.

Before going on to the final step, I allow the glaze to dry partially until it becomes sticky. This is very important since I want to both blend and scumble paint over this glaze in Step 4.

Step 4. Flake white is added to my palette. I take the white and brush this into the glazed pinfeather area, following the direction of the pinfeathers as I work. I allow the underpainting to show through, giving me a nice variation of tones throughout.

With the basic color, I darken the tip and then blend this up into the white. I also add this color sparingly to the outer edge of the feather and blend it up into the pinfeathers, again being careful to follow the direction of the established brushstrokes. The center vein is darkened and a streak of white is placed along the upper half of it, illustrating both curvature and highlights.

My final touch is to paint on a few random spots, so characteristic of feathers. To do this, I use a 1/8″ to 3/16″ sable brush for dabbing on the basic color thinned with painting medium.

24

Indian Beads

Beads play a varied, vital role in the native American's culture. They are used to ornament hair, headdress, clothing, footwear, weapons, blankets, and banners. They bring design and relief to the basic solid colors of Indian hides and leathers. Before machine-woven and printed cloth, beads were one of the few graphic possibilities used in Indian wardrobes. Worn as heavy necklaces or bracelets, they are a dramatic expression of Indian personality.

Beads have great symbolic power. Little worlds or suns, depending on their opaqueness or transparency, beads are a reminder of the heavens' vastness and man's finite place in a limitless universe. Medicine men use beads to administer mysterious cures; historians, to tell the story of the race; artists, to represent Indian truths and beauties. Indian men, women, and children wear beads for adornment and as reminders to themselves of who they are. Beads constantly reinforce the ideal of full communion with nature.

Beads are also valued as counting and record-keeping devices in most cultures. They are used to toll prayers and measure incantations. Or they may stand for the years of a person's life and number of earthly possessions.

Beads, then, serve complex purposes. Just as complex is the technique we use to realistically portray opaque and transparent Indian beads in oil. In fact, this may be the most difficult demonstration in the book to emulate successfully. But repeated attempts will bring satisfaction when you master one of realistic painting's toughest challenges.

The important physical characteristics of beads to keep in mind before starting this demonstration are that light rushes through transparent beads and bounces off opaque beads. With this concept in mind, do the opaque and transparent beads simultaneously so that you can compare differences and similarities of techniques for obtaining the contrasting subtleties involved.

You'll find it will be well worth the effort. There is nothing like a well-painted bit of realistic detail such as a transparent bead to draw the eye into a painting. Then, you appreciate that this high realism is a fine contrast to the more leisurely, relaxed passages. Indian beads surely make for more poetic Western paintings.

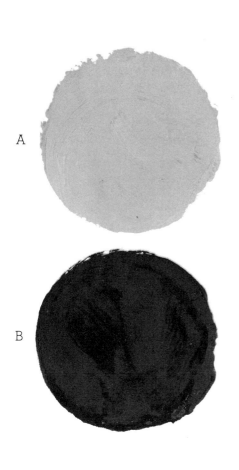

A

B

Step 1. The opaque bead I am rendering is on top in all four steps, and the transparent bead is on the bottom. For ease in identifying each bead from now on, I will refer to the upper bead as A and the lower bead as B.

The texture and essence of both beads will, of course, change dramatically by the end of Step 4, but they will be essentially the same color as in this step. I am using my basic palette of tones #0 to #4, mixed by blending raw umber into a combination of flake white and underpainting white. I begin by rendering two flat, round circles representing each bead. Tone #1 is used for A and tone #4 for B.

Step 2. I have selected a background color of tone #3, and lightly blend both beads into this. Tone #2 is painted into the lower area of A and into the upper area of B. I do this to establish the light source, which is from your right to left. Notice in each bead that a strip of the basic color has been left between the #2 tone and the outer perimeter. The reason for this is that when the light source creates an extreme, be it shadow or light, on a rounded form, the peak of intensity is at the near edge — just before the form rounds out of view. In the case of a shadow, we call this a "form" shadow that always requires blending, as opposed to a cast shadow that ends abruptly.

Step 3. I am carefully blending the #2 tone added in Step 2 upward into bead A and downward into bead B. The darkest portion of the shadow on A is illustrated by placing a strip of #3 along the lower edge of the shadow, blending upward into the #2 tone. On the lower left portion of B, I blend in #2 to render the same reflected backlighting as in bead A's light perimeter below the shadow. In the upper right area of B, I dab in a highlight of #0 or white. Finally, I blend the perimeters of both beads more carefully into the background.

Step 4. This is the step in which I create the transparent look of bead B. Step 3 must be completely dry before I can do this, so I'll finish bead A, which is all wet-in-wet, or impasto, and then go on to discuss bead B.

For bead A, I carefully blend all the tones together, including the highlight in the upper right area. The reflected light along the lower left perimeter is softened by blending it into both the shadow and the background. I now have the finished round, opaque look I'm seeking.

For bead B, I first brush heavy painting medium over the entire bead and surrounding background. Next I lightly glaze raw umber over the bead and background and even over the bright highlight.

From now on I'm working with flake white mixed with a lot of copal concentrate so it's suitable for overpainting. With this white, I dab in the highlight in the upper right portion, leaving the area immediately surrounding it dark. I glaze white in at the bottom, which is the lightest area, and blend upward toward the dark area around the highlight. In the same way, I glaze white around the perimeter, blending smoothly, being sure not to interfere with the dark around the highlight.

DEMONSTRATION 4

Bearskin Robe

An American King. Oil on canvas, 29″ x 33″ (73.66 x 83.82 cm). Everything about this study reflects the regal bearing and attitude of this Indian in the traditional regalia of the chieftain. All parts of the costume are significant, but I feel the bearskin robe is of particular interest. It adds an extra aura of strength. The white areas of the bearskin on the right side represent the skin being exposed where the fur bends. Collection Charles Macaluso.

Bearskin robes and other furs and skins were vital for keeping Indians warm indoors and out. Once away from the campfire in winter — even inside the tepee or hogan — low temperatures meant that everyone had to bundle up unless engaged in intense physical activity. Of course, not every woman and man had a luxurious bearskin robe like this one. It required great bravery to stalk a bear, and not enough of the massive animals were taken to provide wraps for the whole tribe.

But a great chief like "American King" (shown opposite), whose major duties were administrative and ceremonial, was sure to have one. The rich-looking fur added to his stature and was a sign of prestige and position. How majestic to see this noble former warrior rise up to full height under his sweeping, ground-length robe. Imagine him gesturing to the horizon in the bright January sunshine, his thick, mahogony-colored garment shining richly. His council and people must have been truly proud of him.

A bearskin is thick and bristly. To paint one, I begin appropriately enough with a bristle brush, which I use well into the painting. Working thinly, I try to feel out the directions of the fur's flow. I continue this textural approach even when I switch to a sable brush much later in the painting. Dragging painting medium and paint over the brushstrokes is my final technique for reproducing bulky bearskin.

When the white settlers also came to prize bearskins, the animal was nearly exterminated. Now bears are few, and bearskins — even at Ivy League football games and on Indian reservations — are fast becoming a mere memory.

Step 1. Using a bristle brush, I paint on a thin raw umber wash, stressing the shape of the robe, its position relative to the head, and the flow of the fur. The flow depends on the way the robe hangs. The subject is standing with his hand on his hip, which explains the varying directions of brushstrokes. I'm leaving a few areas white for the exposed skins — common in bearskin — which I'll develop later.

Step 2. I begin by brushing in very heavy strokes of underpainting white, which I will need in Step 3 to help me capture the look of fur. I do this in all the lighter fur areas, but not over the skins. In the medium dark areas, I heavily apply an approximation of tone #2, which I also use for the background. Up to now, I still use a bristle brush.

For the areas of exposed skins, I change to a sable brush and an approximation of tone #1. I use raw umber for feathering the fur into the background and for all very dark areas. Also, I brush raw umber lightly across the skins, so the fur will look like it's fluffing across them. I strengthen the facial features, fill in the hair and pigtail, and define the waistline. Now I wait a few hours for the paint to get sticky before going on to Step 3.

Step 3. I'm now using 1/2″ and 3/4″ sable brushes — 1/2″ where the fur requires more delicate rendering and 3/4″ where a rougher appearance is more desirable. My approach is two-fold in this step. I drag raw umber mixed with heavy copal painting medium over the top of and into the existing brushstrokes to capture the furlike texture. Because of this dragging method of applying paint, light areas randomly appear. If they look good, I leave them. This is what is known as "controlled accidents." When I'm satisfied with the furlike effect, I consider the fur finished and darken the hair and pigtail to complete the demonstration.

Arm Wrestlers. Oil on panel, 29″ × 41″ (73.66 × 104.14 cm). The strained expressions on the faces of the cowboys and the tension of the muscles in the hands and arms make up the focal point in the upper center of the painting. The animal skin on the floor, the dog on the far right, the boots, the leather jacket on the figure on the far left, and the vest on the figure on the far right are all tones of brown in which raw sienna predominates. The ultramarine blue jeans and the neutral background allow your attention to go straight to the vibrant reddish skin tones of the cowboys. Collection Dr. and Mrs. Wayne Ramsey.

Old Pete. Oil on canvas, 20″ × 20″ (50.8 × 50.8 cm). This study of an aged cowboy I find typical of this type of individual. Notice the calm, satisfied expression on his face, combined with a very alive, inquisitive look in his eyes. I chose to frame him in an oval to help illuminate this constant flux of moods. Private collection.

Wichita Maiden. Oil on panel, 20″ (50.8 cm) octagon. The raw umber glaze in the background is worked into the full color of the beads and softened into the hair with a finger. Her shoulder is only indicated. This light, delicate touch is just as difficult to create as doing a complete painting. As a matter of fact, some people just simply cannot achieve it, and I would be remiss not to say so. The main thing here is the beadwork, which is probably the most authentic in this book. I really take too many liberties to satisfy the nit-picking realist on details, but in this painting, almost everything in the beadwork is authentic. Private collection.

The Cowboy's Bride. Oil on panel, 18″ × 28″ (45.72 × 71.12 cm). In this study I hoped to reflect the woman's role in Western life. Note the ready adaptibility from range activity — as indicated by her riding clothes flung casually on the chair — to the beguiling softness of a bride-to-be. This transition is punctuated by the flowing folds of her wedding gown and the softness of the veil. Collection Dr. Paul Andresan.

Pardners. (Opposite page) Oil on canvas, 36″ × 60″ (91.44 × 152.40 cm). The cowboy on the left is one of the few characters whom I didn't see fit to change. I have a habit of changing the nose, mouth, or something to suit myself. But this ranch foreman from Abilene with the cigarette dangling from his mouth typifies the tough, lean character you expect to see in a Hollywood movie. His partner in the background is totally made up. Not many cowboys smoke pipes, but I always feel that art is more important than strict authenticity, and I needed that touch of interest of the light from the match and the hands to round out my composition. Collection Diamond M Museum.

Tough Hombres. Oil on canvas, 30″ × 40″ (76.2 × 101.6 cm). The title of this painting reflects the toughness of these range riders that extends even into their leisure time. Of particular interest, aside from the facial expressions, are the blue jeans, the fringed jacket, cowboy boots, and hat, all of which are an integral part of this painting's mood. Collection Diamond M Museum.

Profile of a Cowboy with a Fur Collar. (Above) Oil on canvas, 16″ × 20″ (40.64 × 50.80 cm). It may be very obvious how much I like fur. I like the softness it lends to a picture. In this painting it does even more — the brown fur and hat serve as wonderful complementing colors to the ivory black and white background. This "colorful" painting is good color strictly because the skin tones in the cowboy's head are brought out by these neutral colors. As my old teacher, Ray Froman, used to say, "Remember that good color is a good relationship of color. Anyone can dab blue next to red, next to orange, etc. Any-

one can do fireworks. All color is no color." Make your neutral colors bring out your vivid colors and use them sparingly. Of course, creating a translucent skin tone like that of the old Masters doesn't hurt. Collection Dr. and Mrs. A. Baldwin.

The Horse Traders. (Above right) Oil on panel, 13″ × 21″ (33.02 × 53.34 cm). This painting typifies a Western scene: the anticipation on the part of the horse seller and the interest of the prospective buyers. Notice also the three different types of cowboy hats as well as a vest, two views of cowboy shirts, and the lead rope on the horse. Collection James Hooker.

A Damn Good Yarn. (Right) Oil on panel, 16″ × 28″ (40.64 × 50.80 cm). This painting revolves around old, white-haired Pete feeding the boys a little Texas baloney. The wrinkled, crackled skin in his hands is what one might expect from a man who has spent all his life in the hot, dry Southwestern out-of-doors. Obviously the man lighting a pipe next to Pete is a store owner or clerk in town — not a cowboy. I created the cracks and crevices in the wooden wall and table for contrast with the shiny white and yellow of the beer mugs. Private collection.

Belt and Buckle

The Cowboy Cavalier.
Oil on canvas, 25" × 30"
(63.5 × 76.2 cm). I chose
this title because of the
cowboy's High Renais-
sance pose and the black
hat (which cowboys very
seldom wear). Because
my basic interest has al-
ways centered on the
Masters of the Renais-
sance, I wanted all
things in this painting to
be secondary to the
"light" or translucent,
glowing skin tones in the
face. The background
blends from brown to
gray, and the circular
motion of the rope over
the shoulder is the most
interesting and unusual
part of this design. An
artist should never be
afraid to take liberties for
the sake of art. Collection
Charles Macaluso.

Belts and buckles in the West are products of a sophisticated
Spanish and Mexican silversmithing and leather-working
tradition that goes back to the European military use of belt
and buckle as armor and carrying strap for weapons. In the
West today, not only do belts support trousers but they are
still used to carry hunting knives, ropes, and sometimes a
pistol. For really heavy-duty wear, there is the gun belt,
which holds not only a six-shooter and holster, but ammuni-
tion and other supplies as well.

Although buckles no longer can be considered armor, they
must still complement the belt in sturdiness. The buckle
does, however, retain the beautiful hammered design from
the past military and heraldic tradition. Cowboys often buy
large, elaborate silver belt buckles that are works of art,
created by a solid group of highly skilled Indian, Spanish,
and white craftsmen in the Southwest. Ornate silver buckles
are most often worn by cowboys dressed up for a night on
the town. But I'm still amazed by the belts and buckles some
wear for grinding, hard labor such as digging fence posts
and irrigation ditches.

In this demonstration I did a typical Western belt with double silver buckle. Both belt and buckle have only a slight design, yet workings on both will often be much more detailed.
You'll note I've approached the definition of belt and buckle
and the buckle's shine very gradually. This is because the re-
lation between old hammered silver and tooled leather is extremely subtle and beautiful. Observe as you follow along
why I perform the task somewhat circuitously. Note that I do
the design on both belt and buckle mostly by implication.
Strangely enough, it's more realistic this way. For this
reason, painting a belt and buckle should help develop your
touch.

This demonstration also shows the interesting area where
belt and buckle meet with the materials of pants and shirt
and come together to pinch the wearer's waist. I think there's
every bit as much expressiveness in the way a belt is tight-
ened as there is in a clenched hand or a squinting eye — if
you're on the lookout for it.

Step 1. Since the portions of the belt and the buckle that I'm rendering are in the curved action position in which they naturally appear on the body, my main objective is to show this action and merely indicate the proper location of the major buckle parts. I draw these in by applying a raw umber wash with a wide sable brush. The two loops on the right side of the buckle are leather portions of the buckle. The loops on the left side — only one of which is drawn in — will be silver. The inner silver loop and the pants loop will be added in Step 2. To outline and clarify the various portions of the buckle, I am using raw umber thinned with a small amount of painting medium. This step is now allowed to become sticky.

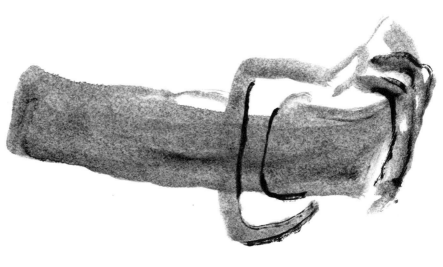

Step 2. I begin by adding to my palette tones #0 to #4 created with raw umber and white. The inner silver buckle and the outer silver buckle are both brushed in with tone #1. Then they are both painted over with tone #2, and white highlights are placed in. The two leather belt buckles on the right are brushed in with tone #1. I glaze in the pants loop with a raw umber wash. To create the rough, leathery texture of the belt itself, I scumble both white and tone #1 into the exposed belt areas. For the dark, differentiating lines in various areas, I use tone #4.

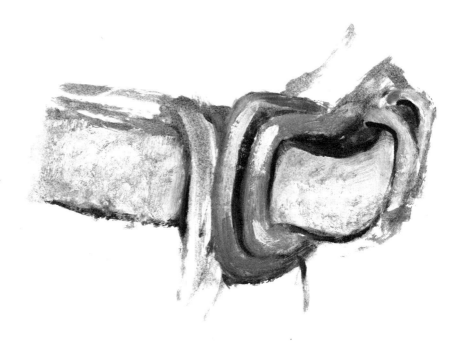

Step 3. I begin to add color around the belt and buckle. On the far right I brush in tone #4 for the background, which fades into tone #1 for the pants themselves. Tone #1 is also brushed into the pants loop. The leather loops on the right are defined by brushing white into tone #1 and then blending raw umber upward from the extreme edges to create a feeling of roundness. White highlights are placed on the top of these two loops. The two silvery buckles both have tone #1 brushed in for a lightening effect, with white highlights added to both. The stitching on the belt itself is rendered by applying raw umber in short, quick dabs with a #2 watercolor brush.

Step 4. I finish off the pants and the pants loop by painting over what is already there with tone #2. The shadow cast by the pants loop is tone #4, as is the background on the far right. I dab in white for the stitching on either side of the pants loop. The two leather loops on the right are roughed in with tones #2 and #3 until they simulate the roughness of leather. The inner silver loop has tone #3 added to it, with a lot of white highlights brushed in. Most of these are blended to create the essence of roundness and smoothness of metal. For the outer silver loop a small amount of tone #3 is again blended in. The dark outline of raw umber at most points surrounding this is lightly blended into the buckle, creating the impression of roundness.

In both the belt and the silver buckle, I seek only to imply design, not to duplicate it exactly. I work both white and raw umber into the belt with a rough touch to simulate the essence of a belt design. The buckle holes in the belt are round dabs of raw umber, with a dab of white added next to each one. The stitching on the belt is dabbed in, with white and raw umber placed alternately. The etched design on the outer silver buckle is created by adding small dabs of underpainting white.

Cowboy's Christmas. Oil on canvas, 24" x 48" (60.96 x 121.92 cm). Ropes or lassos can be used in unlimited ways. This is an example of rope not only used tautly to pull an object but hanging loosely from the saddle. Collection Pal's Cabin Restaurant, West Orange, New Jersey.

DEMONSTRATION 6

Lasso

Rope is the number one tool around horses, cows, and corrals, just as it is for hoisting sail, lashing cargo, and tying up aboard ship. In fact, cowboys might be called "prairie sailors," so alike are the adventurous callings. Both require navigation, coping with unruly elements, fierce independence, the toughest kind of hard work, and, of course, knowing how to handle rope.

A powerful symbol, rope speaks of spotting calves for branding, lassoing wild horses, rodeo riding, lariat tricks, and foreboding nooses thrown up by mob and law alike in the Old West. Today, when much ranching is done by Jeep or Land Rover, there's still no substitute for a rope wielded by hands experienced in working cattle.

To become experienced in depicting Western gear, we should feel and look at rope extensively. In painting rope we cannot overemphasize its roughness or, due to its twists, its series of highs and lows, which are very difficult to reproduce. We can never capture its pronounced texture literally, only its essence. For this reason this is among the most skillful tasks we'll perform in this book.

To paint this lasso, I switch from sable brushes to bristle, then back to sable. Watching the drying of the paint is critical at one point. Basically, I take care not to blend too much in defining the rope's twisting highs and lows. And I do a lot of dabbing and stippling to try for rough texture. Rough glazing, followed by semidrying of the glaze, precedes partially removing it while sticky so I can then work up to an even rougher texture. The painting is completed by a dragging process to create highlights.

Because rope is slender, there's no field or background against which it will make a strong statement when painted alone. For this reason, a lasso must be painted well against a dark background for it to be an arresting feature of any Western picture.

Step 1. I'm using the usual four tones made from raw umber and underpainting white, and I'm working with sable brushes. With tone #2 thinned with turpentine, I paint in the general shape of the lasso. Then, using broad, flared strokes, I capture the casual, loose feel of the knot. For the dark, recessed areas of the knot I use tone #3.

Step 2. The background is tone #4. I fill in all the indented, recessed areas of the rope and knot with tone #3. Then I go back and place tone #1 on all the raised, light areas. I make sure that very little blending takes place. With tone #2 I feather the frayed, straggly ends of the knot into the dark background.

Step 3. I now switch over to a bristle brush. The first thing I do is combine tones #0 and #1 and brush this mixture into the raised areas of the rope and knot. I then dab and stipple flake white into the lightest areas to achieve the rough-textured appearance. As I do this, some of the dark, recessed areas are partially obliterated, enhancing the ropelike effect. I also use this dabbing and stippling procedure on the knot. I am able to reproduce the rope's frayed appearance by allowing my brush to overlap into the background slightly, but not blend into it. The same is true for the frayed area of the knot. Before I continue, this step must be left to dry completely.

Step 4. First I glaze raw umber mixed with lots of painting medium over the entire background, rope, and knot. Then I let it dry a bit so that I can achieve a scumbled effect later. This drying process takes several hours; it's important to allow the paint to reach a sticky consistency before proceeding. Notice how the simple art of glazing gives it a rough, ropelike texture. This is because I painted the rope roughly, so the raw umber glaze would fall naturally into the crevices caused by the brushstrokes. This creates the controlled accident.

Using a dry, flat 1/4" sable brush, I rub over the ridged parts of the rope and knot to remove part of the glaze. Due to the stickiness of the glaze, the effect is that of a very rough texture — exactly what I want for this lasso. In the semishadowy areas, such as the end of the loop, I leave the glaze almost as is. To emphasize the highest and lightest portions of the rope and knot, I mix flake white with a minute amount of raw umber and dab or drag this into the appropriate areas. I lightly brush this same very pale off-white color with a #2 watercolor brush into various spots in the dark background to create the frayed strands of the lasso.

DEMONSTRATION 7
Moccasin

Pueblo Boy. Oil on canvas, 16" x 20" (40.64 x 50.8 cm). This young Indian boy is holding in his hand an object with a leathery exterior. The technique used to render the object is basically the same as that which I used to render the moccasin in this demonstration. Private collection.

Moccasins lend Indians their own special character, just as boots do cowboys. The way in which a man or woman walks "expresses" the man or woman. In the case of the cowboy, his boots give him a certain proud sway and swagger as well as mark him as a horseman. The Indian, gliding along in moccasins, creates his or her image of supple, athletic strength and the quiet efficiency of the outdoor creatures that Indians know so well.

The moccasin gives this sleek impression for good reason. Added to the naturalness of nearly going barefoot is the silence provided by the soft, flexible leather. The heelless slipper, tied on to become part of the foot, received its name from the Algonquin tribe.

Wearing moccasins, Indians can run at great speed, stalk silently through dry leaves, or walk easily upon the snow's crust. You would think moccasins leaky and little protection in winter. Just the opposite seems to be the case. In areas near Indian territory, people other than cowboys—who swear by boots—adopt moccasins for year-round work and play.

The moccasined foot in this demonstration is topped by a ruffled leather pant leg, fastened just above the picture area. The uneven color of the moccasin leather comes from repeated wetting and drying in every season. My technique for this look is to control color depth by varying the amount of medium used with the primary leather tone.

Foot configuration, not obvious when painting shoes or boots, must be taken into account in rendering and painting moccasins. The particular foot involved gives the moccasin its shape, so you must paint moccasins as though feet are inside them. Make sure you indicate ankle, instep, muscles, and toes.

Here, the dark beaded area of the instep adds strongly contrasting elements that can be rendered with simplicity and flair.

Step 1. I'm using my standard four tones made with raw umber and underpainting white and a sable brush for this step. I begin by taking tone #2 and brushing in the basic shape of the moccasin. Besides this I paint in the shoestrings and a couple of prominent wrinkles. Some of the wrinkles are darker than others. This variation of color depth is controlled by the amount of painting medium used with the tone. Additional wrinkles are placed on the side of the moccasin, and I also indicate the moccasin's sole. For the dark instep, I outline the shape with tone #2 and then fill it in with raw umber thinned with painting medium.

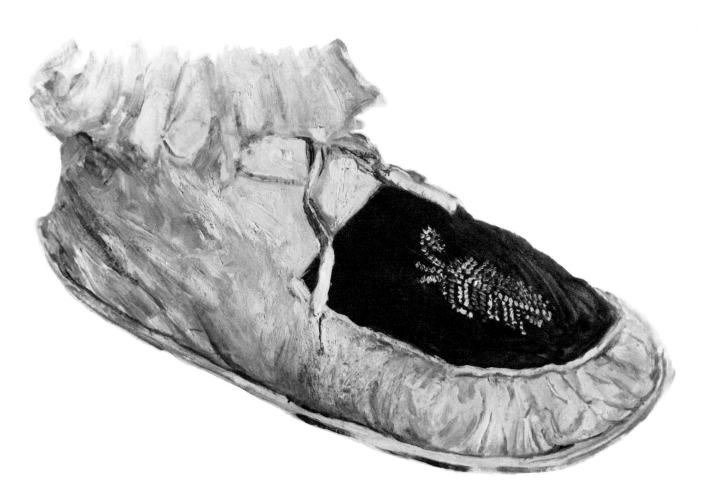

Step 2. I begin by darkening the instep with more raw umber. Next, using a #2 watercolor brush, I dab in the beadwork thickly with underpainting white. I make sure that the paint remains thick as I work because it's important that this beadwork be raised when I finish dabbing. Next I mix an off-white tone by combining tone #1 with underpainting white. I use this to scumble over the shoe area with a bristle brush. Then I blend and scumble tones #2 and #3 into the wrinkles with a sable brush. I also brush these same two tones into the heel portion of the moccasin. Using a #2 watercolor brush, I paint in tone #4 to show the division between the moccasin and the sole. Finally, I define the shoestrings more fully with tone #4.

Old Friends. Oil on panel, 15" x 30" (38.1 x 76.2 cm). Many elements are evident in this painting, but the most important here are the boots that the card tosser is wearing. His boots are in full view and include the toe highlights as well as the tooled detail of the leather in the upper portions. Collection Dr. and Mrs. Burton Tucker.

DEMONSTRATION 8

Boot

Boots give cowboys a lot of their character. The precise, stilt-like way cowboys walk is the result of high heels and so many working hours astride a horse. When cowboy and boots finally touch ground, they are on relatively unfamiliar territory. Required are caution and a conscious thinking out of where they're going and just how to get there, for boots are more steering and prodding tools in the saddle than smooth striding footwear on terra firma.

Like the saddle, the cowboy's other major leather possession, boots vary in appearance from dried out and cracking to smooth and well-oiled, from a cloudy, mulled sherry to a magnificent, rich brandy. Appearance depends much upon care. The same boots that look so parched and worn on the range can, after an application of saddle soap and neat's-foot oil, be worn proudly in the poshest Southwest restaurants. Today's boots can be any kind of material. My own favorite pair happens to be elephant hide dyed black.

The boot in this demonstration, depicted with working jeans, is old and well cared for. Oiling and buffing will bring out, over its whole surface, the same lustrous shine I indicated on the toe.

My treatment of the boot starts with an initial glaze to establish the shining smoothness of leather. In the rest of the demonstration, I brush and blend to roughen the boot to a less glistening texture and add the stitched design to provide a nice contrast with the jeans. I do this very simply by brushing underpainting white and raising the stitch with a thin line of raw umber for shadow.

Crevices and roundness are very important to the boot. Both are accomplished by more attention to smooth blending than usual. The raw umber background blended into the back of the boot, and the straight raw umber shadows under the toe and arch, are vital to complete the boot's roundness and the appearance of standing firmly on the ground. The resulting well-made, well-designed boot is a reminder of the cowboy's appreciation of craftsmanship, so necessary in his self-reliant profession.

Step 1. In this step I'm only using raw umber mixed with painting medium. I don't mix my tonal values until Step 2. Using a 3/8″ flat sable brush, I paint in the outline of the boot. In order to maintain perspective and relationships, I'm drawing in an upper portion of the boot, just to show it's there. However, in the rest of the steps the bottom of the jeans will cover this area. With a very thin wash of raw umber and painting medium I fill in the boot, leaving the lightest areas white. I indicate the boot's wrinkles and shadows and paint in the shadows under the toe and arch with straight raw umber. These two shadows are very important because they give the boot the appearance of standing firmly on the ground.

Step 2. The four tones I use in this step are created by mixing raw umber and underpainting white. I'm working with a natural curve bristle brush. I use tone #3 on the toe and then paint #1 between the toe and the instep, blending them slightly. Tone #1 is brushed into the uppermost part of the instep. The semidark areas, such as the instep and the heel, are tone #2. As I work in all these areas, I randomly allow the glaze to show through, thus enhancing the rough-textured feel of leather that I'm trying to capture.

To render the deep crevices around the ankle, I first fill in the shadowed portions with #3 and then blend upward. I use tone #3 for the vertical seam, making sure it follows the curvature of the deep folds in the leather. The sole and the wooden heel are a combination of tones #1 and #2 applied separately. The shadowed area where the sole joins the boot is rendered with #4, as are the two shadows on the floor. My final touch here is to place a white highlight on the toe, simply to remind me that it's there.

Step 3. The most prominent task in this step is rendering the stitched design on the boot. Before tackling this, however, I blend and refine all the areas of the boot, sole, and wooden heel. As I do this, I naturally lose some of the roughness of Step 2, but this is of no major concern. I make sure to maintain the highlight on the toe.

After being satisfied that the lights and darks have been properly emphasized and blended, it's time to paint in the design. I draw in the design with a water-color brush loaded with underpainting white, brushing it simply into the existing paint. The stitching is raised, of course, so to render this, I paint thin lines of raw umber next to the design in several places. It's not necessary to paint the raw umber next to every stitched line, nor to follow any line to completion. Occasional use of the raw umber provides the necessary impression. I blend the raw umber background into the back of the boot to indicate roundness. This step must now dry completely before going to Step 4.

Step 4. In this final step I only work with two colors: raw umber and flake white. I form a glaze by diluting raw umber with painting medium and glaze this mixture over the entire painting. The glaze skimming over the previously painted brushstrokes is what creates the texture of worn leather here. In the areas I want to depict as lighter than this, I take a dry brush and remove some of the glaze.

In the large highlighted areas, such as the area between the toe and instep, the instep itself, and the large fold around the ankle, I scumble in flake white, blending it somewhat. Flake white is also used for the bright, sharp highlights such as on the toe, design, and seam. Where the sole joins the shoe, I paint in additional raw umber and blend upward to accentuate the form of the boot. For the background I use more raw umber, blending in white as it approaches the toe.

Cowboy's Friend. Oil on canvas, 24″ x 36″ (60.96 x 91.44 cm). The cowboy on the range has many things he depends on, but food takes on special importance in the wilderness. The call to "chow" used by the cook is typical and is made of metal like the spur. I apply the same technique here to render the firmness of metal with its characteristic highlights. Collection Pal's Cabin Restaurant, West Orange, New Jersey.

DEMONSTRATION 9
Spur

Spurs are spiked wheels cowboys wear attached to their boots to urge their horses forward. Jingling spurs tip off everybody on the cowboy's whereabouts. Introduced to the West by Spanish and U.S. military riders, spurs are scorned by Indian horsemen. The native American's strength is being fast on his feet and lightninglike getting on and off his horse. Spurs and boots considerably hinder this kind of speed.

But there's poetry in the sound of spurs when a band of riders cross a mesa or as a lone cowboy trods the main street of a west Texas town late at night. And spurs aren't sadistic medieval torture instruments like the mace or battle-ax. Spikes have become rounder over the years as people — on one level at least — have become more humane.

Spurs are precision made from a high-strength, silver alloy. They have a fine craftsman's look about them so typical of Western artifacts, both Indian and cowboy. The wheel itself has a cold brilliance I took pains to define in this demonstration.

Although the hardware cannot be seen in the finished step, the manner in which spurs are attached to the rider's heels has much to do with the way cowboys position their feet when they ride, walk, or relax. I made an initial sketch of the ordinarily hidden straps and buckle to make sure I caught the correct feeling of a spurred and booted foot.

The picture is done in a thin wash technique with liberal use of painting medium. This provides maximum contrast between the darkest darks and the final shiny, highlighted areas of the spiked wheel. To keep this vivid look of etched metal, I devote special care to blackening portions of the wheel next to these highlighted areas.

A cowboy in full regalia doesn't have much chance to forget who he is and what he does. He is constantly reminded by the sound and feel of spurs — the chiming tools of his trade.

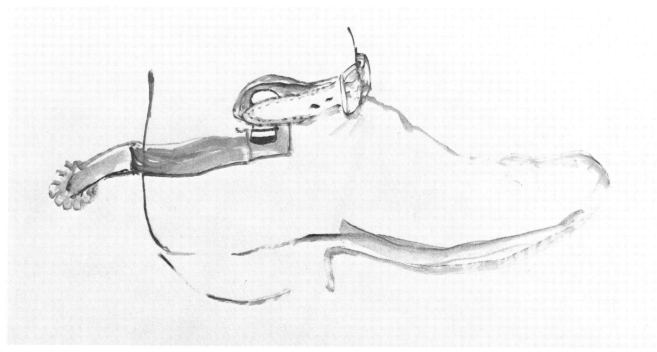

Step 1. This first step is visually different from the other steps because here I'm exposing the securing straps and buckle of a spur, which are always covered by chaps or pants. The reason for this is that I feel it's important to be familiar with an entire entity and be able to visualize it's workings, rather than to be solely concerned with what is visible.

I'm working with a 3/8" flat sable brush. The tones I'm using are created by adding white to the basic color obtained when I mix raw umber and ultramarine blue. Working exclusively with a wash of tone #3 and painting medium, I paint in the outlines and proportions, including the boot so as to establish relationships. The darker lines are created by using less medium with tone #3.

Step 2. Here I render the subject again to show the chap covering the spur and boot, with the blue jean exposed through the V opening in the back of the chaps. Continuing to work with tone #3 in wash form, I fill in the spur, the extension between the spur and boot, and that portion on the boot itself. For definition of the dark areas, such as along the lower edge and around the knob attaching the spur, I apply tone #3 more thickly and use practically no painting medium. The white showing through on top of and between the two spur extensions is the white of the surface on which I'm painting.

Step 3. I begin by painting in a background of tone #3, leaving blank a tiny area around the spikes and the top edges of both sides of the extension to show depth and establish a light source. To emphasize these light areas I come back in with white, using a #2 watercolor brush.

The body of the spur is etched metal, and to establish the pattern, I use unthinned tone #3. I come back in with thinned-down tone #2 in spots where the basic wash over which I'm working appears too dark. I fill in the heel and add wrinkles in the chaps and blue jeans.

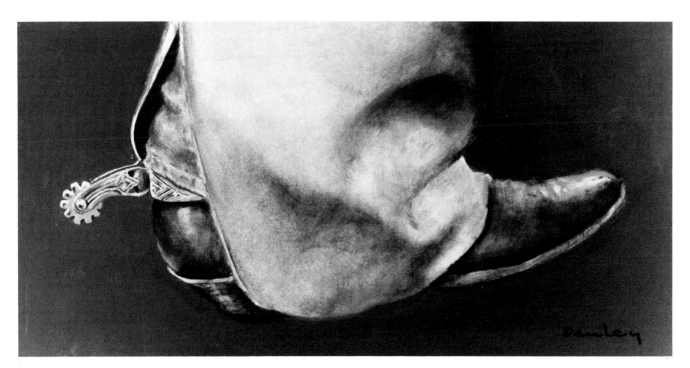

Step 4. This is the final step where I achieve the look and essence of silvery metal. To render this successfully, it's important to retain sharp contrasts. There may be slight blending, but letting the colors relate sharply to each other is the most common technique. For the basic silvery color, on the flat unetched surface, I use tone #2.

The shiny highlighted areas are white, with the other tones used where needed. Notice that I frequently place a very thin, dark line next to a highlighted streak to indicate the light hitting the upper rim of a groove. I complete the boot, chaps, blue jeans, and background to set off the spurs.

Down from the Pass. Oil on canvas, 39″ x 68″ (99.06 x 172.72 cm). In this painting, I show highlights in the eyes, hair, and the bit in the horse's mouth. They are rendered much the same as the highlights on the pistol. Private collection.

DEMONSTRATION 10
Pistol

Cowboy pistols, or six-shooters, won the West. In the vast territories, it was every man for himself. Many felt the need to pack protection normally provided by society in the city. On the frontier's wide-open spaces, shelter was sometimes little more than a flimsy lean-to. Cowboy and pioneer had to be ready to defend themselves against unscrupulous men and untamed beasts of all descriptions. The revolver was policeman, fence, front door lock, and insurance policy. Always within fingertip reach, pistols were an absolute necessity in a land abounding in snakes, cougars, wolves, and human predators.

Today, guns are worn much less by cowboys. Now, with the country tamed, it is in the city where real danger lies. So unless cowboys head into rocky areas where rattlers are found or expect to spend the night sleeping under the stars, they are usually as unarmed as an office worker. And when cowboys do strap on six-shooters, they're not often the gorgeous, old, long-barreled model in this demonstration.

What's needed to render this solid-looking old weapon is getting the look of roughly forged steel and the worn wooden handle — the appearance of age from a time when most everything was more customized and smacked less of the assembly line. Also to be kept in mind as you paint are the cold feel of metal and the warm touch of wood.

Like any well-designed machine, such as a locomotive or a clipper ship, if you're to paint it realistically, you must render it carefully or the result will be unconvincing. A pistol is a detailed, somewhat complex piece of hardware. You must work it up carefully. I use a light wash approach here. Shadows, reflections, and highlights are sometimes subtle, sometimes dramatic on formed steel. So I use one careful blending technique not used elsewhere in this book — grading paint with my finger. Texture of the handle is simulated by a scumbling technique. This starts setting up the look of pitted, grainy, dried hardwood.

The graduated cylindrical chamber and barrel receive mass and reality by careful attention to shadow, highlight, and blending. A successful painting of the cowboy pistol will make the viewer want to pick up the gun to test its weight and balance.

Step 1. In this demonstration in particular, Step 1 is very important. All parts of the pistol must be accurately rendered, proportions must be exact, and the relative positioning of each part to the surrounding parts must be correct. For this rendering I'm using raw umber with painting medium mixed to the consistency of a wash. I lightly render all the visible parts of the pistol and allow this to get a little sticky before doing Step 2.

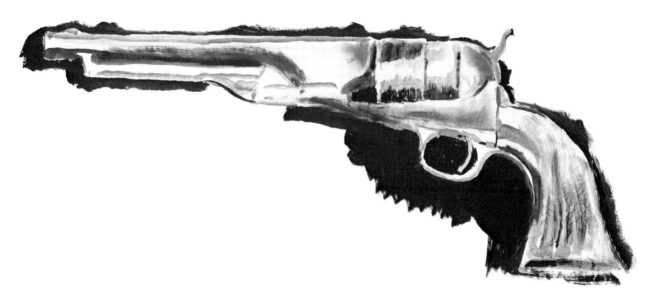

Step 2. The only change I'm making as I work on this step is that I'm now working with raw umber mixed with much less painting medium. I outline the pistol with raw umber and fill in the dark vacant spaces on either side of the trigger. I then paint in thinned raw umber to indicate the medium-toned parts of the gun, such as the hammer and part of the cylinder casing. Sometimes I blend the paint with my finger, such as in front of, behind, and below the cylinder. Then I continue working in the darker areas.

By lightly dragging raw umber back and forth on the handle, I begin simulating the texture of wood. Next, I concentrate on accenting the dark, prominent portions of the gun, such as under the barrel, on the top and bottom of the cylinder (to denote roundness), in the darkly shadowed area just in front of the cylinder, and in the dark slot in which the trigger moves.

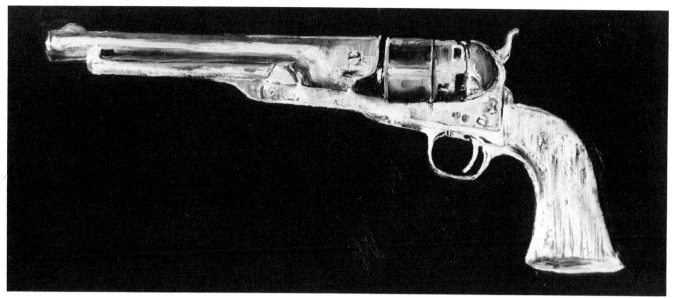

Step 3. I'm adding underpainting white to my palette. In this step I'm filling in all areas with paint and refining and mottling what I have. Using a bristle brush, I streak white into all the lightest portions, such as on the long highlight on the barrel and cylinder, under the cylinder, and into the wooden handle. I also add the screws, such as at the back of the barrel and above the trigger. Raw umber is streaked roughly into the handle to establish the essence of wood.

To create roundness on the barrel and cylinder, I brush in raw umber above and below the middle highlight, blending it into the middle tone where necessary. This is also done in the rounded area just in front of the hammer. Then I fill in the solid dark areas with raw umber and complete the raw umber background. I let the paint dry completely after this step.

Step 4. In this final step, I'll be working with the body of the gun, and after it's completed, I'll finish the handle. Generally, I want to keep the work fairly rough, to maintain the character of a pistol, yet smooth enough to appear finished. Because of this double objective, I'm using soft sable brushes and applying my paint very thinly in order not to destroy the underlying brushstrokes.

First, I lightly glaze raw umber over the whole body of the pistol, except for the handle. I allow this to become sticky. Next, I glaze over all the white or highlighted areas with flake white, blending it into the sticky raw umber for softness. After that, I strengthen the very dark areas with more raw umber.

To complete the handle, I glaze over the wood with raw umber and then wipe it off with a soft brush and painting medium. This emphasizes the grain of the wood. To further highlight the grain, I take a very small sable brush and remove more of the glaze along the edge of some of the cracks and crevices. This produces the soft highlights created as the light hits these areas.

Color
Demonstrations

Golden Raindancer. Oil on canvas, 40" x 48" (101.6 x 121.92 cm). This painting illustrates several typical parts of the Indian's costume. It combines both light and dark feathers in the headdress, both long and round beads, metallic ornaments, a spear, and an animal skin fashioned into a shield — all of the utmost importance to the rain-activities. Private collection.

Because of its unique role in America's history, the West has a romantic, fascinating allure. Besides the mighty grandeur and awesome beauty of the land, the rich and varied heritage of the West is full of heroes of all descriptions. It's no wonder that Western people offer exciting opportunities for interesting character studies. In each of the six demonstrations that follow, each subject is portrayed in a manner and style that is in keeping with the great traditional painters as well as with the culture of the West: the revered Indian elder, the young Indian warrior, the lively Indian maiden, the innocent Indian child, the modern-day cowboy, and the experienced range rider.

Twenty Dollar Joe

An Indian in full manhood holds more than a few problems for an artist attempting an Indian portrait for the first time. His bone structure, features, hair, and complexion are all distinctive. But most challenging is his "attitude" or personality, formed by centuries of living close to nature on the hills and prairies. His eyes have a deep gaze. Like a clear pool, they reflect the look of skies, storms, and bounding prey. Perhaps that tinge of sadness wasn't always reflected in his countenance. Maybe it developed from the change in his lifestyle imposed on him by the new and different civilization surrounding him.

When painting Indian portraits, I make sure to put in highlights, shadows, and middle tones in much richer, darker hues. At the same time, I leave myself an opening to go back and pick up the interesting burnished skin tones that are so different from the Caucasian's pink and gray skin colors. Besides high cheekbones and Indian facial traits, there's something else not always captured by artists — the irregular, rough-textured Indian skin. This skin surface invites design and offers the artist the possibility of the "controlled accident."

For this skin color and texture I use transparent gold ochre for a darker key tone than the usual raw sienna. Indian red is also a good pigment to use here. Blue-black Indian hair calls for raw umber and ultramarine blue, with a later glaze of ivory black. I usually paint the backgrounds of Indian portraits with ivory black and white or some painting medium and raw umber to reinforce the skin color.

The face of the Indian accepts the high-keyed brightness of the sun more readily than does that of the Caucasian. Light and weather are kinder to the Indian skin, and wrinkles are less pronounced until old age. I paint the wrinkles with this in mind, softening them by blending.

Re-creating the Indian isn't the work of a moment. Only by repeated attempts have I learned to paint Indians, and in so doing, I've made several good friends.

Young Indian Man

Young Indian warriors were called "braves" for good reason. They fulfilled extreme tests of courage and endurance before taking their places in tribal armies. Besides fighting and riding skills, Indian men had to learn to hunt and skin, to survive alone on the trail in below-zero weather, and to give and receive blows without whimpering. In addition, they made, and learned to use, their armaments and tools — bow and arrow, hatchet, and tomahawk. All this was in preparation for major displays of fearlessness that warriors were required to perform.

Today, young male Indians are tough, hardy, and proud of their inheritance. They work at hard, daring jobs in U.S. industry, such as steeplejacking and on towering construction. And when it comes to idealistically fighting for Indian rights, militancy is still alive, with Wounded Knee testimony to their hardy spirits.

Young Indians, like the one I painted here, often have lighter complexions than their elders, whose skin has turned copper-colored from age and weather. In the younger male, there's greater contrast between skin color and jet black hair than there is with their fathers and grandfathers. I've emphasized this by balancing highlights between shining hair and forehead, and cheekbone and chest. Hair highlights are blended from raw umber and white.

Much of this painting's effectiveness depends on a glaze made with raw sienna and medium that is used over the face, neck, and chest to re-create delicate skin transparency. While this glaze was sticky, I brushed over it with a mixture of burnt sienna and flake white. The gray whisker area was defined with a mixture of ivory black and white. I believe the result is a sympathetic portrayal of a young man who looks proud of both his manhood and his Indian heritage.

Laughing Girl

An Indian woman's beauty lies in the contrast of her rich, satiny, blue-black hair with her sparkling white teeth. These two elements play across her face to bring lively, exciting harmony to her naturally burnished complexion. With these contrasts in mind, I proceeded with this portrait, much of my planning already done for me. Of course, as far as beauty is concerned, it doesn't hurt to have my model's exquisitely fine features and wonderful grooming.

Unifying this portrait are the highlights, more prevalent than usual in a painting. They reflect the strong Southwestern sun in tones that ascend to white. These highlight areas are so numerous and pronounced because of the subject's classical, smooth facial contours and skin. To convey this, I begin with a smooth painting surface. I choose Masonite covered with gesso rather than a rougher, stretched canvas.

I adjust my palette somewhat from the male Indian portraits to render the naturally lighter-skinned female Indian. Eliminating Indian red, I keep raw sienna, raw umber, Venetian red, cadmium red, and gold ochre, and add cadmium red deep. Ultramarine blue and raw umber are basic for her hair. Underpainting white and flake white are also used, as well as ivory black.

I start skin highlights by removing originally applied raw sienna with painting medium. The contrast between black hair and white teeth is bridged by highlights and whites of the eyes, and the painting explores the darker and lighter qualities of her skin tones. Because my subject is lighter-skinned than her male counterparts, her shadow areas are relatively darker. Therefore, the painting was a process of tightening the darks and lights on the subject's smooth, subtle skin.

I gave particular attention to establishing the tone and expression of her smiling eyes and mouth. Achieving that made this Indian woman come "alive" on canvas.

Pueblo Child

An Indian child's life today is far different from when his forebears roamed the plains, mountains, and valleys. Parents may retain much of the tribal culture, but the child's upbringing has changed radically.

Once, little Indians were carried wherever mother and father went — as a papoose on mother's back or trailing father's horse in a sled of crossed poles and leather carrying basket. Now, children are indoors much more of the time. Days are spent by mother's side, or, as more Indian mothers join white women working in an industrialized society, Indian children are often in day care centers until school age.

Even though these changes may eventually transform revered Indian ways, modern life hasn't yet masked the frank, clear-eyed look of young Indian children. Their exceptional gaze is the subject of this painting, which is done in a thin technique on gesso-covered Masonite. I was fascinated by the eyes of this very young model, who has the honor of being the great-great-grandson of a well-known chieftain.

I develop his deep-welled eyes with a raw sienna rendering. Pupils and eyelashes are black made of ultramarine blue and raw umber. The whites of his eyes are flake white blended with just a trace of black. A faint Venetian red and white blend is painted along lower lids and inner corners of the eyes. Irises are done in transparent yellow ochre, and then with a mixture of yellow ochre and white. Pupils are highlighted with white.

Though my subject will never suffer the rigorous life of his forebears, he has ever new and changing horizons to conquer. His trusting gaze indicates the existence of time-honored strength necessary to overcome the challenges of the future.

Young Cowboy

Young cowboys, like the rest of the West, are changing. Although their job is traditional—they are still close to land and cattle, and their many skills and work practices are the same as those of a century ago — the men themselves are affected by urbanization. Good roads, fast cars, and small planes that tie in ranch and city are making them a new breed. They are exposed to education, new ideas on TV, and the cultural life of big city centers. Some are troubled and rebelling because of the exposure. They wonder where their place really is. Now they must decide between new careers and bringing back the best of the cosmopolitan world to enrich cattle raising. But young cowboys also realize a ranching investment can be profitable and it's healthy to live the rigorous cowboy life.

It is this modern, defiant, cultured look that I've tried to capture in this painting of the young cowboy. His hairstyle has changed. His habits have changed. He does a lot more thinking. There's "a burr under his saddle," and he's not quite sure how to get rid of it. Some of the time he's glumly silent, and there's a chip on his shoulder. That's this particular young cowboy.

The stark contrast in his face — fully lighted on one side, shadowed on the other — emphasizes the dual, conflicting forces working upon him. The light side of his face is begun in a yellow ochre and white mixture over the basic burnt sienna and white skin tone. The shadow side is a combination of raw umber, ultramarine blue, and the same brown mixture used for his hair.

I give the thinking, somewhat troubled eyes special attention. Irises are the same gray used for the whiskers. Then I add raw umber to them, and later, black, ultramarine blue, white, and medium. Pupils are a black made from raw umber and ultramarine blue. Whites of the eyes are white plus medium, then toned down with white blended with a trace of black. Medium and white are also used for highlights in the eyes. Venetian red is added subtly along the eyelids.

Young cowboys aren't all Hamlet-like, tragic princes. But this range rider seemed like one to me. That's why I painted him this way.

Weathered Cowboy

Cowpokes, as they ride the range, are constantly exposed to the elements. After twenty years, a man looks much older than you'd suspect from the date on his birth certificate. In this painting I stress the result of this weathering through one of its contributing forces — the high-keyed light of the Southwest. Although this is a picture of extreme contrasts across most of the painted surface, it also calls for subtlety in portraying the dignified trail rider. Perhaps it requires more subtlety than most character studies because the eye is forced by the vivid contrasts to contemplate the more finely worked halftone areas.

This might be called a study of deep neck crevices because they are shown in a most revealing light. The work required more paint build-up than usual for projecting highlighted features like the nose and eyebrows. On the other hand, paint was applied thinner than usual in the darkest shadows to make sure they receded proportionately.

Skin tones always call for all the subtlety a painter can muster. I found this weathered subject, in this light, a special challenge. I brought about the result by a combination of glazing, tinting, and overpainting.

This is not a soft-skinned face. It's just the opposite. In most lights it would look dark and leathery. But not here. The sharp Southwestern light pouring in unlocks delicate shadings more likely to result from a lifetime in drawing rooms, rather than on cattle drives. But it does not unlock them all. Just here and there. That's what gave me a special interest in the "Weathered Cowboy."

Twenty Dollar Joe

Step 1. The only two colors used in this step are raw umber and flake white. I combine these colors to create a basic color for underpainting. I can make this basic color lighter or darker by changing the proportions of the two colors that I mix. In this way, I create different tones — lighter or darker than the basic color. I use Taubes copal painting medium light combined with some copal varnish for my own painting medium.

With a sable brush, I begin to paint in the various tonal values, beginning with the darkest values and ending with the lightest. This produces the essence of my subject and provides a good painting base.

I surround the head with a background of raw umber and flake white thinned to the consistency of a wash. I work until I feel satisfied that I have captured the tilt of the head, features, and costume as well as reproduced the correct values. Then, at this stage, I set the painting aside for a couple of hours. The paint should dry until it reaches a sticky consistency before beginning Step 2.

Step 2. While the paint is still sticky, I take a large sable brush, dip it into my painting medium, and then into transparent gold ochre. This color is similar to, but darker than, raw sienna. I can now brush this color very lightly over the basic skin color without smearing it, because it is not easily disturbed.

I mix raw umber and ultramarine blue to create a black that I use for the hair, brow, and pupil of the eye. I also brush this color lightly into the whisker area to produce a greenish effect over the yellow skin-colored base. Next I take Indian red and brush it lightly into the facial areas, mostly in the cheek, nose, and chin. I blend this color lightly. By now the paint should be getting quite sticky. So I take a bristle brush loaded with underpainting white and cover the areas of the portrait that will be very light or white. The sticky underpainting allows me to get a rough, scumbled effect.

As I add these colors to the face, I'm establishing the essence of my character's appearance without worrying about delineating every crevice. With this approach I'm actually creating "controlled accidents" that will ultimately produce a more relaxed, natural-appearing painting. If I find the face too pale, I add more of the red, yellow, or black to compensate.

At this stage, I change the background color with Winsor & Newton raw umber and white. For the furry edge of the shawl part of the costume, I use my black made of raw umber and ultramarine blue. I paint in the beadwork and design on the shawl with ultramarine blue and black. Then I render the right-hand sleeve with raw umber.

Step 3. I now switch to heavy copal painting medium that I mix into Venetian red. I use this glaze on the nose, cheek, ear, chin, and a couple of spots on both the upper and lower eyelids.

Next I mix my painting medium with transparent gold ochre and glaze the entire rest of the head except for the eyeball and the mouth, which I shall treat separately later.

I use Indian red mixed with this heavy medium on the shawl. To provide a good color to contrast with the skin tones, I use my medium and raw umber over the entire background. Again, I allow the paint to become quite sticky before I continue to Step 4.

Step 4. All the colors that I use from here on I mix with heavy copal painting medium. I begin by glazing ivory black over the hair, except for its highlight, which I further enhance with flake white. This same flake white is what I use to work into the glazed red areas. Due to the stickiness of the red, I can push it into the paint already there to produce a semiscumbled effect at some points and a smoother, glazed effect on other portions.

Next I mix a gray from black and white, which I work into the wrinkles, nose, nostrils, ear, cheekbone, and jaw, blending as I work. This gives me a variation of color depending upon which color base I work it over. In other words, the gray will be a different color on the nose than it is on the whisker area. After completing this, I add white highlights in areas such as the nose and neck, taking care not to blend, since these should be sharp highlights. I complete this step by glazing raw umber over the beads and design on the shawl.

Step 5. The paint should be very sticky — not quite dry — before adding final touches. With a large bristle brush, I paint raw sienna into the yellowish portions of the head. Taking the same type of brush, I work Venetian red into the reddish portions in varying degrees. I keep working these two colors in until I achieve the skin tones I want. Then I take a sable brush and apply cadmium red to emphasize the very red areas such as the cheek, nostril, and ear. By working the paint in this manner, even though I've actually scumbled and glazed, I ultimately achieve a wet-in-wet look.

I add black to the eyebrow. Yellow ochre and white are combined and brushed into the forehead, cheek, nose, chin, and throat. I also use it for the highlight on the chin, and I soften all the wrinkles by blending.

To complete the eyeball, I use a sable brush and work ivory black into the pupil. Then I glaze raw umber into the iris and add a touch of yellow ochre and white next to the pupil to achieve luminosity. The mouth is completed by combining Indian red and white to form a cool pink.

I indulge in artistic liberties in this step by adding a large fur collar; I introduce this to enhance the skin tones, through contrast. To render the fur I use my black made from raw umber and ultramarine blue, brushing gently into the background for softness. I paint in the ribbon around the pigtail with oxide of chromium mixed with a lot of copal concentrate, while I render the outer edge along the neck and the divisions within the ribbon with the black of raw umber and ultramarine blue. I blend this into the skin tone to avoid harshness. For the background I use black-and-white gray and a large amount of painting medium brushed on with a large sable brush.

Young Indian Man

Step 1. My palette consists of three colors: raw umber, ultramarine blue, and flake white. I mix raw umber and white to create my five basic tonal values. To create black I mix ultramarine blue with raw umber in a 50/50 ratio.

After my preliminary brush-in of the features and the tilt of the head with thinned-down tone #1, I mix white with the black and fill in the background.

Using my black, I paint in the hair, brushing into the background as I work in order to create softness. The highlights in the hair are tone #2 blended softly into the black. The pupils of the eyes, eyebrows, eyelashes, and forehead shadow on the subject's right are also black. The rest of the head is worked in with the five basic tones.

For the fur, I use white for the skins and brush into this my black, which I mix heavy on the raw umber side. I also feather this off into the background to add to the furlike effect. I render the shirt with the same black mixed with white for a gray and then add a white trim.

Step 2. I add raw sienna and Venetian red to my palette. During this step I don't touch the hair or eyes. This is a glazing step, so no white will be used at this point.

After the fur has dried, I glaze raw umber over the fur and lightly over the skins. I continue to work the raw umber outward from the back of the furpiece into the gray background. I also glaze raw umber into the shirt, taking care not to touch the white edge.

I mix painting medium with raw sienna and brush this over the entire skin tone except for the lips. The glaze is brushed on thinner where the light hits the face — such as the left side of the forehead, by the left eye, the left eyelid, and on the chest.

I strengthen the shadow areas with raw umber and glaze Venetian red over the lips for the final touch in this step.

Now I let this step dry until the glaze becomes sticky.

Step 3. Now I add burnt sienna, ivory black, and yellow ochre to my palette. I mix burnt sienna and flake white together and brush this mixture over and into the sticky glaze of the facial area with a ⅜" brush. Where I desire the reddish tones to be more prominent — such as in the nose and cheek areas — I come back in with just the burnt sienna. I also brush the combination of burnt sienna and flake white into the lips, toning them down to a more nearly natural shade.

I create a gray by mixing ivory black and white together and work this color into such gray facial areas as the whiskers and the left side of the subject's left eye.

I mix ultramarine blue and raw umber together for a cool black, which I brush into the eyebrows, the sockets of both eyes, and the deeply shadowed right side of the face. On this deeply shadowed right side, I use raw sienna as the blending agent between the lights and the darks.

I brush white mixed with yellow ochre into the highlight areas on the forehead, nose, cheekbone, lower lip, and chin. To finish the eyes, I glaze raw umber over each iris with a soft sable brush. Then with a #2 watercolor brush, I touch a little raw sienna next to the pupil for a translucent look.

The fur is finished by glazing a little more raw umber into it, in the same manner as that described in Step 2, in order to darken and enrich it. I also brush a bit more of the raw umber into the background for added effect.

Laughing Girl

Step 1. My palette consists of raw umber, raw sienna, ultramarine blue, and underpainting white. After capturing the basic shape and tilt of the head and features with thinned-down raw umber, I use raw sienna for the basic skin color. I develop the lighter areas, which are the highlight areas, such as the center forehead, cheek, and nose, by brushing in light copal painting medium with a sable brush to remove the desired amounts of raw sienna.

For the shadow areas, I lightly brush in raw umber. I also use it for the eyes and brows. As I paint in the hair shadows on the left side of the face, I allow the shadows to convey the curvature of the face.

The lips are raw umber. I use underpainting white for the teeth and raw umber for the delineations between the teeth and their shadows.

Raw umber mixed with a small amount of ultramarine blue is the hair color. This combination produces what I term a "warm" black. I create the highlights by using painting medium to remove the color in the same manner as that used for the facial highlights.

I use the hair color thinned considerably for the background. I draw in the costume and beads with thinned raw umber.

Step 2. I'm adding flake white and Venetian red to my palette. Also, I'm adding more ultramarine blue to the warm black hair color on the palette to create a cool black.

I brush flake white into the unshadowed areas of the face. I apply it more thickly in the lighter areas and more thinly in the darker areas. I take some of my cool black, mix it with raw sienna, and use this for a greenish shadow tone. I brush this into the shadow areas, such as the cheeks, chin, and alongside the right eye. The cool black is what I use as a gray middle tone between the right eye and nose, and on the bridge of the nose. The eyebrows are cool black lightly brushed into the skin tones. For the irises I apply a combination of raw umber and raw sienna.

Next, I use Venetian red on both lips, mixed with a little white on the lower lip. For that lip's highlights I use flake white. I also touch Venetian red into the inner corners of the eyes and the left nostril. The teeth shadows are cool black blended into the teeth.

I brush cool black over the hair and hair highlights, which I emphasize with white mixed with a little blue. I apply a cool gray mixed with white and blue for the collar. I use the greenish shadow color for the dark areas of the background, blending it around the head.

Step 3. First I add ivory black, cadmium red deep, cadmium yellow deep, yellow ochre, and cerulean blue to my palette. I lightly brush cadmium red deep, blended with flake white, into the lips. Then I carefully blend cadmium red deep into the reddish areas of the face — primarily the cheeks, nose, and around the eyes. A very small amount is used on the chin and none at all on the forehead. To darken the hair, pupils, eyebrows, and lashes, I delicately brush ivory black into these areas with a sable brush.

I paint in the cape with ultramarine blue, using raw umber for the folds and the shadowy lower portion. I add white for the highlights on the shoulder. The bright yellow part of the costume flowing down her back is rendered with a combination of raw umber, raw sienna, and cadmium yellow deep, which I work in to create the appropriate highlights and folds. I use these same colors for the gold in the beadwork. The red beads are cadmium red deep with white highlights, and the paler beads are ivory black and white mixed with a little yellow ochre. The turquoise at the bottom of the beadwork is cerulean blue. Nothing further is done to the beadwork. I blend the colors in both the blue and yellow portions of the cape to give a softer finish. For the background I mix raw umber and my warm black and blend this into the cool black I used in the lower left corner.

The background is now completely black.

In this last phase, which could be termed a tinting and glazing process, all work is done with a sable brush and heavy copal painting medium. I add transparent gold ochre, burnt umber, and cadmium red light to my palette.

First, I lightly blend transparent gold ochre into the forehead. Next, I blend burnt umber into the following shadow areas: between the subject's right eye and the bridge of the nose, along the outside of the right eye, between the underpart of the right nostril and the right side of the upper lip, and into the right cheek hollow. Also, I brush it into the mouth opening, the shadow areas of both lips, under the lower lip, into the right portion of the chin, and finally on the subject's left cheek by the mouth.

I brush in a combination of burnt umber and ivory black around the outer portion of both irises. Around the pupils I work in raw sienna mixed with painting medium to produce a glossy effect. I use ivory black for the pupils and eyelashes. I add cadmium red light to emphasize the lower lip. For the final touch, I mix ultramarine blue and white, which I lightly brush under the chin on her right to indicate a reflection radiating from the clothing.

Pueblo Child

Step 1. This painting would be less effective if done on canvas, so I chose Masonite covered with gesso. It is a thin painting technique that I seldom use, except for women and children. I'll be working with sable brushes, and in this step there are only three colors on my palette — raw sienna, ultramarine blue, and raw umber. I combine the latter two to create a black.
My initial concern is to render the proportions, accurate location of the features, and basic character of my subject. I loosely define the hair with my black thinned with painting medium. The outlines of the face, eyes, and the entire mouth are rendered with raw sienna. I use black for the pupils of the eyes, but mix black and raw sienna for the outline of the nose, shadow indications on the left side of the face, and the shadows on both sides of the mouth.

Step 2. I add Venetian red to my palette. I paint a thin raw sienna glaze over the entire face except for the eyes and mouth. To depict the forms and shadows on the face I use raw sienna mixed with much less painting medium. The lips are rendered with Venetian red, which I also apply lightly on the lower lids. I use black for the eyelashes, nostrils, lip separation, and the shadows on either side of the mouth and under the lower lip. I define the hair considerably by adding more black to what is already there. Before proceeding I let this step become sticky for a period of 3 to 4 hours.

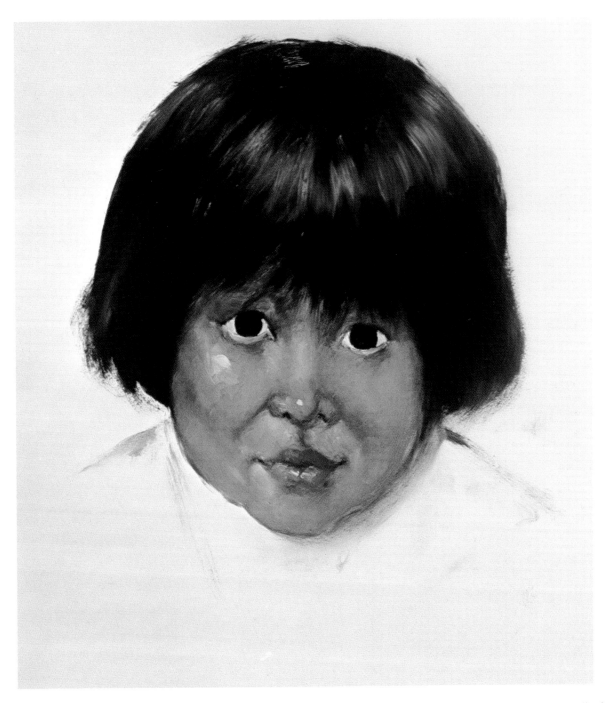

Step 3. I add flake white and yellow ochre to my palette, which I mix together to create a pale yellowish white. I brush this color into the entire skin area to create skin tone. It's applied more thinly in the dark, shadowy areas, allowing the underpainting to show through, and it's thicker in the light areas, such as the bridge of the nose, cheeks, chin, and upper lip where a lighter color is desired. Any dark areas I wish to accent, such as the cupid's bow on the upper lip, are rendered by adding raw sienna and blending this well into the yellow ochre and white combination.

As for the eyes, the whites of the eyes are flake white toned down with a tiny bit of black for a nice off-white color. I paint in a pale combination of Venetian red and white along the lower lids and in the inner corners of the eyes. I also combine Venetian red and white for the mouth, with a small amount of black for the lip dividing line, corners of the mouth, and vague outline of the upper lip.

For the highlight on the lower lip, I use white, while the highlights on the nose and the right cheek are a combination of yellow ochre and white. The hair is fully rendered with black, its highlights with white.

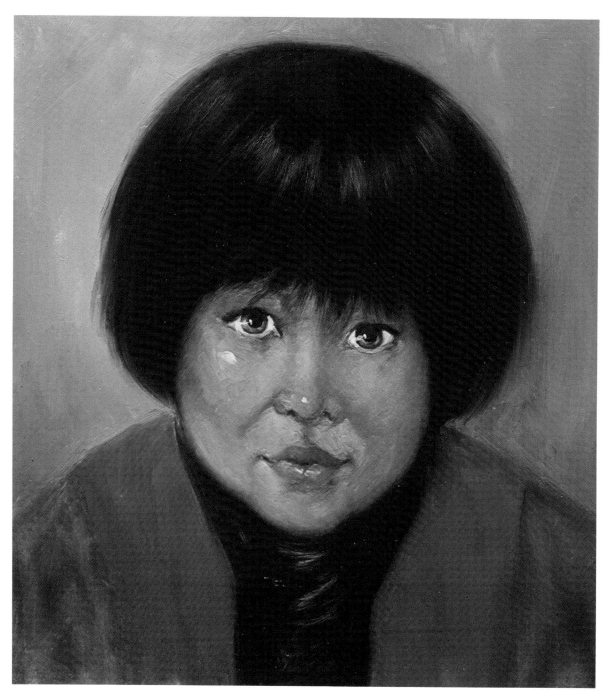

Step 4. Here I include ivory black and Indian red on my palette. I mix ivory black with flake white to create the gray for the background. I glaze ivory black over the hair and remove it in the highlight areas with a dry brush. This creates the toned-down highlights over certain portions of the hair. Also I brush the outline of the hair back and forth into the background, creating an aura of softness.

From this point on, the black referred to is that which I mix from ultramarine blue and raw umber. To complete the eyes, I paint black into the eyelashes. The pupils of the eyes remain black while the irises are rendered with transparent yellow ochre. A yellow ochre and white combination is also painted into the irises to create additional lightness. White is used for the highlights on the

pupils. On the lower eyelids and in the corners of the eyes I use a combination of Venetian red and white.

On the right jaw I also use the yellow ochre and white combination to provide extra lightness, since this is the lighter side of the face.

I paint in the red of the vest with Indian red. The sweater over which the vest is worn is a dark brownish black, so I use my black, highlighted with raw umber, for the center portion as well as the neck. To maintain softness around the facial outline, the black of the sweater is blended up into the jaw along with raw sienna. Black enhances skin tones, so this gives me a good chance to use this factor to my advantage. I paint in the sleeves of the sweater with raw umber.

Young Cowboy

Step 1. My palette contains burnt sienna, flake white, raw umber, ultramarine blue, cadmium red deep, and yellow ochre, and I'm working with bristle brushes from ¼" to ¾" in width during this step. I mix burnt sienna and white together in varying degrees of light and dark to paint in all the facial skin tone, even the lips. Raw umber, ultramarine blue, and white are mixed together for the gray I use in the whisker area and along the far outer edge of the right cheek. I use this same gray to render the hat and shirt. The eyebrows are painted with the same gray, but of a darker value. The shadows around the nose are also the same gray with a small amount of burnt sienna mixed in. With the addition of white and occasionally raw umber, I also work in the gray for the background. The vest is also gray, but very thickly painted on. I use this thickness to help create the heavy texture of this item. The bandana is painted in with cadmium red deep and my black mixed of raw umber and ultramarine blue.

I create the brown tone for the hair by mixing burnt sienna, ultramarine blue, and yellow ochre. Yellow ochre and white are combined for the highlights on the hair as well as on the face. The deeply shadowed areas such as under the hat and on the right side of the cowboy's face are rendered by mixing raw umber and blue with the brown used for the hair. The gray that I use in the whisker area I apply for the irises. For the pupils I mix black from raw umber and ultramarine blue.

Step 2. With a sable brush and raw sienna I glaze over the entire face, excluding the mouth and eyeballs. I mix black from raw umber and ultramarine blue and use this wherever black is needed in this step: around the eyes, in the eye sockets, for the eyebrows, for the heavy shadow on the right side of the nose, on the depression between the nose and the upper lip, and under the lower lip.

I touch in raw umber for the irises of both eyes, leaving the pupils black. I paint white mixed with copal painting medium into the eyeball with a sable brush. Now, this step must sit until sticky.

Step 3. I add ivory black and Venetian red to my palette. Using a bristle brush, I mix yellow ochre and white and paint this into the light facial areas, such as the forehead, eye sockets, nose and cheek highlights. I mix Venetian red and white together with the same brush for the reddish areas, such as the nose, left cheek, chin, and part of the right cheek. This combination is also worked into both lips. I paint a black-and-

white gray into the whisker area, the right side of the face, and around the left eye.

I touch Venetian red into the corner of the left eye, along the lower lid, and also along the lid of the right eye. I also dab it into his left cheek.

I complete this step by painting a thin raw umber glaze over his hair. Now I let this step dry completely before proceeding.

Step 4. The black I've mixed from raw umber and ultramarine blue I mix with the black-and-white gray for the background. I blend the hair into the background using raw umber on the man's right side and raw sienna on the lighter left side.

I lightly paint my blended black into the shadowy right side of the face. I work raw sienna along with Venetian red back into this area.

For the irises of the eyes, I work in my blended black, adding ultramarine blue to it along with white and copal concentrate. I brush this gray color into the irises with a #2 watercolor brush. The pupils are my blended black. I paint the whites with white toned down with a small amount of black. I use copal concentrate and white for the highlights in the eyes.

To complete the hat, I glaze over it with raw umber and then come back with raw sienna, using white for the highlights. The shirt is glazed over with black; then I go over it with white for the very light areas. I use raw umber and raw sienna for the vest, with highlights of yellow ochre and flake white. Finally, I glaze over the background with black.

Weathered Cowboy

Step 1. In this beginning step, I want to capture only the shadows because they are so prominent in this likeness. Since they are cast shadows, that is, shadows created as light is blocked off by a neighboring shape, they are rather sharply defined.

I combine raw umber and flake white to create a color that I can work with comfortably to capture all the shadows. A sable brush is a help in applying the paint thinly, which is important in this early stage.

I paint in the deep crevices in the neck with alternating strokes of raw umber and flake white. A very slight degree of blending may inadvertently take place but it isn't necessary. I begin all deep crevices in this manner, even those appearing in later steps of this painting.

Step 2. Various combinations of raw umber and flake white are what I'm painting with exclusively in this step. I want to accurately capture all the lights and darks that appear in the face, blending where necessary as in the chin, cheek, and nose areas.

The deep crevices you see all over the face were begun in the same manner as were the neck crevices in Step 1. I continue blending the raw umber and white back and forth until all the crevices are well blended.

For the small detail work I use a #2 watercolor brush; I prefer to use a Grumbacher Rubens series because it points well. A 1/4" or 3/8" sable brush is what I'll use for the remainder of the face.

In the very light-colored areas, such as the nose and eyebrows, I allow the paint to be applied very thickly, but I want the paint to be thin in the dark areas, such as the inside of the mouth and the pupils.

I render the shirt and the suspenders with raw umber and white, blending to capture the folds and shadows under the collar. The background is a raw umber glaze. Now the painting must be left for at least two days to completely dry before proceeding.

Step 3. I add Venetian red to my palette. This step is exclusively devoted to glazing. I take Venetian red mixed with heavy copal painting medium and glaze very thinly over the entire face and eyeballs, taking care to avoid the eyebrows, sideburns, and cigarette.

Next I mix a lot of heavy copal painting medium into Winsor & Newton raw umber to make it very thin, and glaze over the background and the hat. I also glaze lightly into the right side of the shirt with the same glaze.

I let the paint sit for awhile to become sticky, but not dry, so it will be workable for Step 4. The combined effect of glazing, tinting, and overpainting can thus be achieved in the following step.

Step 4. I add ivory black and raw sienna to my palette. With a sable brush, I brush and push small amounts of flake white into the sticky Venetian red on the face, producing a semiscumbled effect in some areas and a smoother, glazed effect on other portions. The raw umber and white tones of Step 2 show through the layers of paint, creating various shades of pink skin tones. From now on I will be enriching these skin tones in various areas to create more depth of color.

I add flake white in a few places, such as the high-light areas on the nose and chin and on the deep wrinkles. Sparingly, I brush in raw sienna in the yellowish areas, such as the cast shadow portions of the forehead, right cheek, and neck.

Next I mix ivory black and white for a dark gray that I use in the beard, chin, cheekbones, and wrinkles. I also use this gray in the eyebrow shadows and the shadow areas of the hair. I conclude this step by using raw umber in the very dark areas, such as the opening in the mouth, in the ear, and directly under the chin.

Step 5. Here I add cadmium red deep, yellow ochre, and phthalocyanine blue to my palette. I mix yellow ochre and white together for the light areas of the face. In large areas I use a bristle brush, allowing the paint to drag, and in the small detail areas I use a #2 sable watercolor brush. I apply the paint very heavily in some areas, such as the highlights on the nose, left cheekbone, and above the left eye, blending slightly as I go. As I work with this color, the general appearance of the skin tone lightens considerably. I now work Venetian red back into the reddish areas.

I brush black-and-white gray into the shadow cast by the hat on both the forehead and the right cheek. I also add gray to the wrinkle areas by bearing down to accentuate the deep wrinkles and applying it lightly to the other wrinkles. When I use this gray in the lighted portion of the subject's face, it's important to confine it strictly to the shadow and whisker areas. I brush cadmium red deep into the cheekbone, lips, and nose as a final touch.

I work phthalo blue and white into the shirt to emphasize its whiteness and to render the shadows. For the suspenders, I use a black created from phthalo blue and raw umber mixed with white. For the hat, I brush in my black to get the dark areas and glaze in raw sienna for the lighter, middle-toned areas. The highlights are phthalo blue and white mixed and brushed into the raw sienna areas. I complete the background by brushing over it with a combination of ivory black and a minute amount of phthalo blue.

Indian Headdress

Indian headdresses are extravaganzas for special occasions. When Indians want to blend with the scenery and slip soundlessly and unnoticed through woods or brush, they leave their headdresses behind.

Great amalgams of fluff, feathers, beads, skins, headband, disks, and feather holders, headdresses are for ceremony, celebration, or full-scale attack by pony soldiers. Tribal government, religious rites, and warfare all call for the proud wearing of brilliant plumage. When ruling councils of chiefs and elders sit, when men and women pray for their crops, good hunting, deliverance from the enemy, or when they take up arms, then is a time to don the magnificence of the headdress.

Indian war bonnets are among the last great adornments worn by males in the 20th century. Once men in many advanced civilizations wore heroic, handsome coverings that provided stirring subjects for painters. For instance, the Dutch masters painted wealthy burghers with soft, plume-topped velvet caps; dazzling, helmeted soldiers; and officials with high, silver-buckled hats. Now, male dress reflects that urban men have become the extensions of machines. For this reason alone, the Indian who maintains his headdress provides an outstanding opportunity for a painter.

Down, or fluff, on which this demonstration concentrates, is collected by Indians from bases or stems of feathers. Large quantities of down from many birds are needed for each headdress, since the fluffy material is the predominant feature.

Other parts of this picture, although important, are not handled with quite as much detail as this fluff. Still, this painting involves a surprising number of different textures, plus the varied techniques needed to render them. That's because our problem is to tie all the picture elements together. The other textures must contrast with and accentuate the fluffy impression we are trying to make. As in Demonstration 2, on the feather, I use a special color rather than the usual four tonal values.

To give you some idea of the alternation of textures I try to set up, here are the varying methods of applying paint that I use to achieve the look of real down in the headdress: glazing, scumbling, dabbing, flicking, raking, and skimming.

Commanche Knight. Oil on canvas, 40" × 52" (101.60 × 132.08 cm). This Indian represents the regalness and dynamic bearing of a past era. The subject is, in fact, a Commanche wearing the time-honored outfit of a past and present chieftain — a feathered headdress, bearskin robe, and beaded belt, among other things. But no matter how well rendered or put together, these items would be meaningless without the proud bearing and expression of this very impressive representative of Indian culture. Collection Governor Dolph Brisco of Texas.

Step 1. The Indian headdress is a mixture of several shapes and textures, all of which I'll deal with in this demonstration, except for the feathers. Their rendering was thoroughly explained in Demonstration 2; for any details refer to that demonstration.

For this demonstration I won't be working with four tonal values; instead I'll use a color created by mixing approximately three parts raw umber with one part ultramarine blue. The only other color I'll use is flake white in the later steps. All my brushwork is done with sable brushes unless otherwise specified.

My first step is to mix my basic color with a lot of painting medium and then just outline the various portions of the headdress and face. What I'm striving for is to capture proportions and relationships. When I'm satisfied with that, I go on to the next step.

Step 2. I mix a thin glaze of my basic color and painting medium and brush this into four areas of the headdress: the headband, the thick down radiating outward from the headband, the circular decoration over the ear, and the skins dangling from this disk. This glaze needs to become sticky before I can proceed since I want to scumble and pull paint into all four areas. As I fill in the downy area, I use short, casual brushstrokes extending into the background to produce the elementary feathery look desired at this time. In this immediate area I also show a few streaks, such as in the lower right, to indicate the stems of feathers to be painted in later.

The animal skins dangling from the disk are rendered by using less painting medium with the basic color, in order to create a darker color. The fluff or down is attached to the headband by a group of decorative feather stem holders. During this step I indicate the shadows between these holders, since they require a darker tone than the holders themselves. I continue to sharpen the facial features and add the outline of a neckpiece.

Step 3. Flake white is added to my palette. I begin work in this step by scumbling short, curved strokes of flake white into the downy area to create the impression of fluff. This is done with a ⅜" natural curve bristle brush. The paint is allowed to build up thickly in preparation for a glaze that will be applied in Step 4. The feathers extending beyond this fluff are glazed in with the basic color. Some of the veins are indicated with streaks of white. In this same area I also fill in a dark background color to allow the feathers to show up more prominently. I render the feather holders at the base of the fluff very loosely, mainly indicating that the sides round into darkness while the front portion is light.

Since the headband and the disk are beaded, I dab on flake white with a ¼" brush. Some of the undertone will show through, helping to create the beaded look. I also dab around the perimeters of both areas with a darker color. The designs on these items are dabbed in with a mixture of the basic color and flake white. I fill in the features and embellish the neckpiece. I allow this step to dry completely before starting Step 4.

Step 4. I mix a thin glaze of basic color and painting medium and paint this over the entire headdress. In the fluff portion, I paint the glaze darker on the right side where it is shadowed. Now I let this glaze dry until sticky, or almost completely dry. Depending on weather conditions, this may take nearly a day.

Next, with a sable fan-shaped brush, I flick flake white mixed with copal concentrate into the fluff. I keep doing this until the fluff appears thick and airy. On the right side, I just barely rake the white over the glaze. The white areas are blended into the darker areas simply by using less and less white.

The feather holders and the large feathers are finished when the glaze is painted over them. Using a sable brush and white mixed with copal concentrate, I lightly skim the surface of the headband and disk, working very lightly over the designs and the area where the headband rounds the forehead. This same white mixture is painted into the dangling skins and allowed to feather out along the outer edges. I complete the face and the neckpiece to finish this demonstration.

Cowboy with a Black Hat. Oil on canvas, 16″ x 20″ (40.64 x 50.8 cm). This is a head study of what I considered a typical cowboy in a black felt hat. Although I've been questioned about whether or not cowboys do wear black hats, I've seen several and this is an accurate rendition. Note the softness used to capture the feeling of felt, even though it's black (which makes this texture more difficult to portray). Of course, black absorbs the sun and is a bit impractical, but it sets off skin tones so well. Private collection.

DEMONSTRATION 12
Felt Hat

An old felt cowboy hat is the symbol of the West. Protection from relentless sun, wind, and rain, it is a soft, pliable complement to the raw, angular features of its wearers. Used for every possible outdoor activity — snoozing under, carrying water in if necessary, and affectionately "whipping" horses onward — the felt cowboy hat becomes part of he who wears it.

Such a hat, like the cowboy on the trail, really takes a beating. Luckily for hat and cowboy, the material, by definition, can withstand it. Felt is an ancient Anglo-Saxon word for the soft, resilient wool material that is "cloth made by pounding or beating." Often mixed with fur or hair, it is worked together by pressure, heat, and chemical action, without weaving or knitting. No wonder it is favored for the rigorous life of the West.

Painting the old felt cowboy hat forces me to relate to the natural simplicity of its manufacture. It also involves techniques that might be compared with the weathering the hat receives.

My colors for the old cowboy hat are only raw umber, underpainting white, and flake white. You might say that I "beat" tones of raw umber and underpainting white into the white Masonite board to make the hat look real, as scumbling is the predominant technique I use to reproduce the texture of worn felt.

Helping a lot to reveal the texture of the hat are the shadows that radiate almost straight overhead in this painting — a light condition common in the Southwest where the sun is high in the sky much of the year.

With this "natural" approach to painting felt, I establish brushstroke patterns and concentrate on these brushstrokes to maintain the "brushy" quality that is the secret of reproducing old felt in paint. Also I continually blend light areas into shadow and shadow areas into background to complete the soft statement that is old felt.

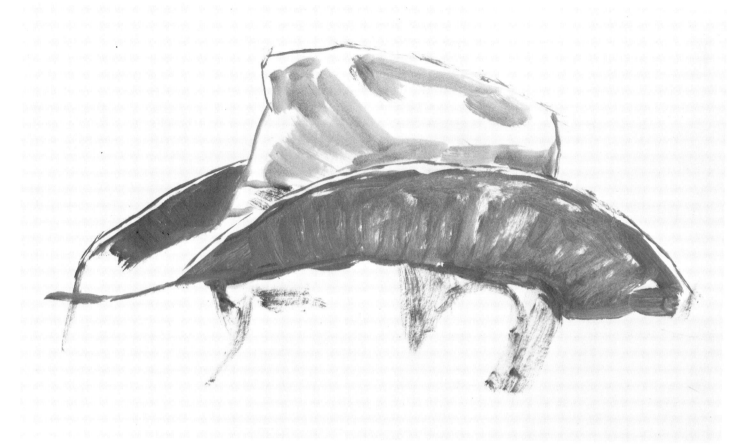

Step 1. My first objective in this step is to capture the drawing of the hat rather than the material of which it is made. I place underpainting white on my palette, and I'll refer to it as tone #0. I then squeeze out raw umber, and I'll refer to that as tone #4. Tones #1, #2, and #3 are combinations of these two colors, varying in strength proportionately between the white and the raw umber. Heavy copal is my painting medium.

For the sake of definition, I shall refer to the long upturned brim in the foreground as the near brim. The smaller portion of brim exposed in the rear will be the far brim, and the area between these two, the center brim. The remaining raised part of the hat I'll refer to as the crown.

The only tone I'm using for this step is tone #2, which becomes lighter or darker depending upon the amount of painting medium used with it. As I begin rendering, I'm using more medium for the light areas and less for the darker areas. The very lightest areas, such as the center brim and outer rim of the brim, I leave unpainted since I'm working on white board. I use hardly any painting medium in the darkest area, which is the far brim. I also draw in the outline of a head with tone #1 thinned down so the hat will be resting on something.

Step 2. My main objective in this step is to fill in all values and to capture the texture of worn felt. I combine tones #3 and #4 for the background so I can blend the shadow areas into it. The other edges are not softened in this stage. To lay the groundwork for the textured look, I lightly scumble both #0 and #1 over the entire hat. I use them separately, sometimes scumbling #0 and sometimes #1.

I then mix a tiny bit of tone #1 into #0 to produce an off-white that I brush into the center brim, the left side of the crown, the dent in the crown, and the rim up to where it fades into shadow on the far right.

Tone #3 is brushed into the shadowed top portion of the dent in the crown. It is also painted into both the near and the far brims. Because the near brim is lighter as it approaches the face, I scumble #1 into that portion. I work tone #1 into the facial area and tone #3 to fill out the hairline.

Step 3. As soon as the paint is thoroughly dry, I glaze tone #4 over the entire background. Next I use painting medium mixed with a minute amount of tone #4 over the entire hat, creating a tint. From now on as I work, I follow the existing brushstroke patterns to maintain the brushy quality so important in representing the texture of leather. I then brush flake white into the lightest areas, which are the center brim, left edge of the crown, dent in the crown, and the rim. Notice that the white appears rather dark because of the underpainting over which it is being applied. The various tones are brushed in elsewhere on the hat to represent the ap-

propriate tonal values.

I blend the shadowed right side of both the near brim and the crown into the background by using tone #4 mixed with a great deal of painting medium. I also glaze #4 into the far brim, softening the edges as I work. I complete the face and upper torso of the figure to give the hat a proper resting place.

The hat can be considered finished at this point or advanced, depending on your preference. If you choose to continue, allow the paint to dry for one day until it becomes sticky.

Riders at Dusk. Oil on panel, 20″ x 30″ (50.8 x 76.2 cm). Here is a painting that illustrates two additional views of the cowboy's felt hat as well as many other items demonstrated in this book. Notice also how your attention is drawn to the glassy eyes of the horses. Collection Charles Connolly.

Lookin' for Strays. Oil on panel, 24" x 40" (60.06 x 101.6 cm). The dust cloud rising as the horse and rider hit the slope of the hill obliterates the hoofs of the horse but provides action in the painting. The chaps, leather jacket, and straw hat are all typical cowboy gear. The scenery in this picture was painted in West Texas near Abilene. Collection Pal's Cabin Restaurant, West Orange, New Jersey.

DEMONSTRATION 13
Straw Hat

A straw cowboy hat in the Southwest provides a natural cooling system. When air starts moving up from the Gulf of Mexico thoroughly baked to searing temperatures, the straw cowboy hat "squeaks" softly as the cowpuncher rides along in search of shade, water, and grazing land.

The feather-light covering is a golden, transparent change for the ranch hand. The hat offers shade in contrast with the dead, hot air under the wide-brimmed felt hat — a much more familiar feature of Western gear. Straw provides enormous comfort at noontime when rattlers pant in the shade of a solitary rock and riders and cattle wend through dry gulches praying for September and the start of the rainy season.

Portraying this kind of hat is as elemental as its manufacture. Straw hats are a loose weave of vegetable material. To paint them, I use a loose weave of paint over the careful lay-in of three simple tones made of raw umber and underpainting white.

Weaving by brush is more properly called the "streaking process." You do this by placing two tones on the brush at once and dragging it along in circular strokes that follow the curvature of the hat. Or two tones can be applied separately with a smaller brush in the same manner.

Most transparent and open in the straw hat is the upper crown where light and background seep through. This part, where the top of the cowboy's head does not reach, is defined in fragile detail by careful application of the darkest tone. Like any different or fanciful headgear, the straw cowboy hat is a real boon for the artist who wants to show off human features. Personality is not only what face or mannerism says it is, but what the subject says about himself by what he wears.

Straw hats provide a satisfying texture in an oil painting. In this picture, the hat holds its own above the twisted, craggy face of our cowboy.

Step 1. I'm limiting this step to drawing the hat and laying in the most prominent shadows. The two colors used to mix tones #1 to #4 are raw umber and underpainting white. Underpainting white is also the white used throughout this demonstration.

I use tone #2 thinned with painting medium exclusively in this step. After I'm satisfied that I have captured the shape, tilt, and essence of the hat, I paint in the hatband and the dark shadows on the far brim and crown. (I'll use the same terminology for hat parts as in Step 1 of Demonstration 12.) I paint in the shadow on the near brim very lightly because considerable mottling must take place in later stages. I outline the head on which the hat rests.

Step 2. I now take tone #1 and fill in all the areas that I left white in Step 1. Along the rim of the hat I brush in white to indicate separation. Taking tone #2, I lightly brush in an expanded and more precise shadow on the crown. The hatband and the shadow on the far brim are reemphasized with tone #2. I use this same tone to lightly blend in the shadow on the near brim. With tone #1 I further outline the head and ear. The background is filled in with tone #3.

Step 3. The rudiments of the straw texture are captured in this step mainly by a streaking process. I begin by streaking both #1 and #2 with a sable brush onto the near brim. Notice that I use circular strokes to follow the curvature of the brim. Then I add streaks of tone #3 on the same brim, using less in the lighter portion near the front and more as it rounds into shadow at the rear and lower areas. The streaks on the crown, center brim, and far brim are done with underpainting white, since these areas are the lightest on the hat.

I brush tone #3 into the rim of the brim to make sure the separation is now visually established. Tone #3 is also used for the design in the upper crown, the deeply shadowed portions of the far brim, the hat band, and the cast shadow on the left side of the band. I paint in the face and outline the upper part of the torso, filling in the collar area of the shirt. This step is allowed to dry completely before proceeding.

111

Step 4. This step is exclusively one of glazing, exactly the same as Step 4 of Demonstration 6, the lasso. I glaze over the entire background and hat with raw umber mixed with a large amount of painting medium. This glaze must be left alone several hours to become sticky enough to allow me to scumble and pull the paint in Step 5. If I proceed too soon, my strokes will blend together and I won't be able to maintain the rough straw texture. For this reason I keep testing the consistency of the glaze before beginning Step 5.

Step 5. To create the streaked look of straw, I begin by taking a dry brush and removing the glaze where I want the lighter tones. The area where this needs to be done most precisely is on the near brim where the streaks are most clearly defined. I leave the glaze where I want dark streaks or dark areas, such as on the rear of the brim. I continue this glaze removal process all over the hat. Where I want stronger highlights, I scumble in flake white, such as on the center of the crown and the center brim. This completes the rough-textured appearance of a straw hat, and I finish the weathered character who wears it.

Warmin' In and Out. Oil on panel, 24″ x 36″ (60.96 x 91.44 cm). These two cowboys by a campfire show different examples of the cowboy's supple shirt. For the sake of comfort, his shirt is always very soft and therefore displays many areas of gentle folds. Collection Pal's Cabin Restaurant, West Orange, New Jersey.

DEMONSTRATION 14
Shirt

The cowboy wears his shirt — be it worn denim or flannel — nice and loose. It feels freer that way — good for sleeping in if you have to on the range. It leaves room for a sweat shirt or thermal underwear in cold weather. The breathing room it allows makes the cowboy a more relaxed individual.

Paintings of the soft, full cowboy shirt should mirror what the shirt stands for and take a nice, free, comfortable approach. I've done this picture very loosely through every step for this reason. I begin by varying the darkness of the shirt's drapery lines with liberal use of painting medium. To get the hard light of the Southwest into this softness, I switched from a soft brush to a bristle brush to dab in flake white. Another contrast to this cowboy shirt's worn softness is the stark darkness in the background.

The cowboy shirt is just another example that a man's occupation will one way or another be reflected in what he shows to the world. It can't be hidden. Our job is to recognize this truth and paint it.

Step 1. I'm working with a soft brush and a wash of raw umber and painting medium in this initial step. I fill in the shirt body and sleeve, striving to capture shape and proportion. To help me do this, I draw in the head, which I use as a point of reference.

Step 2. To indicate the collar, shirt front, pocket, as well as fill in the dark hollows of the wrinkles, I use raw umber mixed with much less painting medium than I used previously. This enables me to control the darkness by adding more or less medium to the raw umber as I see fit. I also further define the head and facial features and outline the top of the legs. Then, I let the painting sit until it is sticky.

Step 3. In this step I use a heavy bristle brush. I brush in flake white so it's thick where I need it to appear the lightest and thinner where it is darker. Where I need a middle tone to either lighten or darken some area, I use a mixture of raw umber and white. To define the buttons, I simply pile up the flake white.

At this point I consider this an artistically rendered shirt. However, if you wish to represent realism more perfectly, simply blend all areas together to create a smoother finish and eliminate the brushy quality in this step.

DEMONSTRATION 15

Vest

Cowboy vests, which are generally made of rough-textured animal skins, provide the protection to the upper part of the cowboy's body that chaps do to his legs. Unless the weather is cold, cowboys do not usually wear jackets. To keep shirt and torso from getting ripped on barbed wire, splintery fences, and cactus — not to mention while wrestling with cows and horses — cowboys wear the tough animal-skin vest.

Besides this protection, the vest gives cowboys much of their elegance and style. Vests have traditionally provided this kind of flair for both sides of the law, a convenient facade for good or evil. Remember how many badges marshals and sheriffs pinned to these cloudy-looking animal-skin garments? On the other hand, how many card sharks have tucked aces, not up sleeves, but in vest pockets? And what about derringers in shoulder holsters beneath vests that have been used to beat enemies to the draw from a seat at the poker table?

Without doubt, the vest was and is an integral part of the attire and lifestyle of the cowboy. Not including a vest on a cowboy in a painting would be an exception, made only for a specific reason. Re-creating the vest in a picture adds a lot to it. Because of its texture, an animal-skin vest provides a pleasing area of poetic looseness, which relieves Western character studies from tightness or rigidity. And the controlled accidents that result from the way I go about painting vests look great. An added benefit is that this method is easy for a skilled craftsman, while ensuring good results as well as practice for those less skilled.

I deliberately placed the cowboy's hand on his waist in this way to add to the character of the vest. The resulting deep shadow inside the vest fold provides the picture's darkest dark, emphasizing the eloquence of the cowboy's attitude and gesture.

The mottled variety of tones of the vest was produced by thin painting, followed by dragging and scumbling into sticky paint. Finally, the look of animal skin is the result of an overall glaze that is partially removed with the brush.

Vests draw the viewer's attention into a cowboy painting. It's fortunate that they are both easy to paint and of a texture that contributes a lot to a picture. (The vest shown here is taken from the complete painting that appears earlier in this book as the frontispiece.)

Step 1. The final result I'm seeking in this demonstration is to fully express the roughness and the animal skin texture of the vest. Aside from what is done in this initial step, the end result is primarily accomplished by glazing and scumbling techniques.

I brush in the basic outline, hang of the vest, and figure with raw umber thinned considerably with painting medium. To add the darkness cast by the right arm and the deep shadow inside the vest fold on the left, I add more raw umber. I let this step now become quite sticky before going further.

Step 2. In addition to the raw umber on my palette, I'm including a mixture of flake white and underpainting white. Since the raw umber wash of Step 1 is now very sticky, I'm able to drag white over the entire vest, with the exception of the black fold on the left. To do this, I'm working with a sable brush heavily loaded with white to produce the thickly painted surface. What happens is that the white and raw umber wash join together in a rough, mottled fashion.

Step 3. Here I scumble over the vest with raw umber, which allows me to produce the variety of tones. For the rough edges of the armholes and neck areas, I flick in white with a #2 watercolor brush and blend it outward into the raw umber background where necessary. I use raw umber to define the seam along the front edges of the vest. I fill in the figure that is wearing the vest. Now this step dries very thoroughly before I begin Step 4.

Step 4. This step is very simple and very quick, but the results make the difference in how well the rough-textured effect is captured. With a wide flat sable brush, I glaze raw umber over the entire vest. Then I clean the brush thoroughly with turpentine and a rag, and I use the same brush to remove some of the glaze. More is removed in the lighter areas and less in the darker areas. Now I have the roughly textured appearance of animal skin, so commonly found in cowboy vests, that gives an authentic look to this young cowboy.

Bush and Matt. Oil on panel, 14″ x 28″ (35.56 x 71.12 cm). My cousin, Bush Ramsey, on the right and his friend Matt have posed for me for several paintings, such as "The Arm Wrestlers," "A Damn Good Yarn," and "Tough Hombres." Neither one of them is what I call a full-fledged cowboy, but living in Abilene, they sometimes look the part. Matt has on a buckskin jacket, which I painted very roughly in this monotone oil. This is one of my "brushier" paintings, which you may or may not prefer to the "slicker" ones. Collection Mrs. W.V. Ramsey.

DEMONSTRATION 16

Buckskin Jacket

The buckskin jacket is an item of Indian clothing that appeals widely to cowboys. The soft, strong, yellowish gray leather is perfect protection for working or riding amid branches and brambles and for crawling or climbing over rocky terrain. In this deer or goatskin covering, the wearer blends with the surroundings — an ability always considered an asset by hunters and trappers, whether Indian or not.

In the past, cured buckskin hides provided serviceable, comfortable clothing far away from urban centers that produced textiles. Today, the dash and utility of the handsome buckskin jacket continue to make it a Western favorite. The swinging tassels provide that relaxed, next-to-nature look.

Buckskin has an extremely even color, tone, and almost a palpable atmosphere like fog or darkness. Besides being ironlike in resisting dmmage, it is so soft it reveals every undulation of the wearer. The problem in painting buckskin, then, is to find and maintain this evenness of tone while creating its porous, mottled look.

Mixing and applying the initial buckskin color are very important. It is nearly impossible to go back to add to or correct the initial application. The color I use is tone #2, raw umber and flake white mixed with a lot of painting medium. What makes things doubly tricky is that the first step must be put aside for about eight hours before scumbling into it with a lighter tone of raw umber and flake white to create the texture. Then the painting must be allowed to get sticky overnight before mottling to add more texture. Later a glaze is partially removed with a dry brush to bring out light-toned areas.

An interesting facet of this picture is that the jacket wrinkles run horizontally where they are pulled across the cowboy's back and vertically where the buckskin falls freely in front. Emphasized for a natural look are the inverted V's of the tassels where the slope changes direction and the tassels split. The shadows under the collar and yoke contribute added subtlety and give the buckskin a softer, richer look.

Buckskin jackets are part of an earlier West — of guides and trail blazers and expert hunters. They're alien to the permanent-press world surrounding us. Paint them with respect and you'll capture the spirit, look, and feel of buckskin.

Step 1. I create four tonal values by mixing together raw umber and flake white. With tone #2 mixed with a lot of painting medium, I fill in the entire jacket, brush in the tassels falling from the sleeve, and outline the face. I'm of course very interested in capturing the shape and proportion of the jacket accurately. But I also want to make sure the jacket area is entirely filled in with paint since this is the initial and a very important step in creating the look of buckskin. After being satisfied that I have completed Step 1, I put it aside until it is sticky — approximately eight hours.

Step 2. I combine flake white and tone #1 together and scumble this over the jacket to create a basic feel of the texture. While doing this, I frequently work in more white to bring out the highlights in all areas. Notice also that in the back and sleeve areas I paint in the direction of the fabric folds. I use tone #3 for the dark areas, such as the shadow under the collar, the yoke seam, and important wrinkles, and for outlining the sleeve tassels. After painting in the yoke seam, I'm able to place the remaining tassels on the back. I do this by using the flake white and #1 combination, with tones #2 and #3 where necessary. Note the inverted V in the tassels by the left shoulder blade. I further define the head and features. This is set aside again, overnight, to allow the paint to become sticky.

Step 3. The work in this step involves a tremendous amount of mottling. I use tones #1 and #2 primarily, on the yoke, back, and sleeve, working in the wrinkles and folds, yet leaving the brushstrokes in somewhat of a rough stage. I brush in the jacket side seam with #2. Notice that the jacket front experiences no stress so the wrinkles fall vertically instead of horizontally. I use various tones to define the tassels. To further define the yoke seam, I stipple the seam with a combination of flake white and tone #1. I place the wearer of the jacket in an appropriate setting.

Step 4. Only raw umber and flake white are used in this step. I glaze over the entire jacket with a thin glaze of raw umber and painting medium. The light-toned areas, such as the top of folds, are depicted by removing some of the glaze with a dry brush. I highlight some of the tassels with flake white. The deep shadows such as under the collar, under the tassels by the arm, between the individual tassels, and in the folds are strengthened with raw umber. The tassels at the bottom of the jacket are completed in the same manner.

Tough Riders. Oil on panel, 15″ x 32″ (38.1 x 81.28 cm). Even though very little of the old man's blue jeans is showing, I have tried to capture their unique qualities and texture here. Notice the paleness indicated in the blue jeans and the seam along the side — so characteristic of this typical cowboy garb. Private collection.

DEMONSTRATION 17
Blue Jeans

Blue jeans and cowboys are inseparable — in more ways than one. Not only do cowboys choose to wear only the coarse blue cotton twills for work and dress, but they wear their jeans tight enough to pop. Around the pens and stalls at Houston's Astrodome during the annual trail ride and rodeo, you'll see well-scrubbed, rock-hard, rail-slim cowpokes in jeans tight enough to cut off circulation from unbelievably bowed legs, the result of a lifetime on a horse. If you can't go West to see for yourself, catch the movie "The Last Picture Show," a classic on today's cowboy.

Why do cowboys wear jeans? Because jeans don't snag or catch when cowboys get in and out of the saddle. They're tough and comfortable, not too hot in summer, and wear- and dirt-resistant. They can be washed over and over again, fading to an appealing shade of smoky blue-white. Another attraction is their informality. These sturdy work pants have recently become a kind of passport everywhere in the U.S.

Jeans' informality is immediately apparent in the large seam on the side of the pant leg. I start this demonstration by following this rippling line in order to capture the liberated spirit of jeans.

In the rest of the painting I concentrate on reproducing the rough-soft, tensed-relaxed look of a leg encased in denim. To keep the material properly faded, and to show muscular structure by means of the shadows and folds, I build from a light initial lay-in of color and painting medium. Later, I emphasize the whiteness of faded denim by scumbling into the partially dried glaze. I achieve the final color, folds, and shadows by blending, mottling, and scumbling. I give particular attention to rendering a blotchy look to the denim and a soft, white appearance to the frayed bottom edge of the pants.

Far from the most glamorous item of cowboy attire, jeans are more a "part" of the rider than anything else he wears. Painting them in this manner will make for a more authentic Western picture. (The jeans shown here are taken from the same painting as Buckskin Jacket, Demonstration 16.)

Step 1. For this demonstration I'm using what I refer to as my basic color, which in this case consists of three parts raw umber and two parts ultramarine blue. I'm not using four tones, but I control the depth of color by the amount of medium I mix in. In this beginning step I'm using a flat sable brush and plenty of painting medium. The seam is the first thing I paint in. The reason for this is that it allows me to have a built-in action line. I fill in the contour of the jean around the seam. I indicate the series of folds behind the knee and lightly brush in the shadow at the back of the leg. I fill in the whole pants leg with a thin wash of basic color and painting medium. As you know, seams in denim become ripply after washing, so to denote this, I place small dabs of paint along the seam. The knee wrinkles are darkened, and I begin detailing other major wrinkles, such as those seen below the knee wrinkles. At the bottom of the leg, I start to indicate fringe by allowing this portion to fan out a bit. Finally, I paint in the beginning background with basic color. I let this step dry almost completely before going on.

Step 2. I add flake white to my palette. To begin mottling the jeans, I scumble flake white over the glaze. When I want to create folds, I push and work the paint in the direction of the folds as I scumble, making sure the darker areas show through and not being afraid to allow the white to be thicker in the lighter areas. I paint white lightly over the top of the seam, allowing it to skip frequently, which maintains the ripply appearance. The fringe is rendered by painting the white on thickly with a small-pointed sable brush. It's important that the white strands be visible. I outline the boot and fill in the background. This step must now dry completely before starting Step 3.

Step 3. I take the basic color and fill in the form shadows, such as the back of the thigh, blending upward along the side of the thigh. The basic color is also worked into the fabric folds. Next, I mix the basic color and flake white together to use in three areas: to mottle the soft folds, to define the seam, and finally to scumble over the paler portions of the jeans, such as the front, to create the rough look of denim. I do this scumbling very randomly, to assure the somewhat blotchy look that is so characteristic of jeans. I mix a very thin glaze of basic color and painting medium and glaze over the frayed edge. Then with a dry brush I wipe some off. Using a #2 watercolor brush, I accentuate the frayed strands with white, and the jeans are completed.

Old Hands. Oil on panel, 28″ x 34″ (71.12 x 86.36 cm). This is my favorite of all my paintings in Pal's Cabin, a restaurant in West Orange, New Jersey. Both men are actually cowboys, though they posed at different times in different places. After initial drawings, I decided to put them together and came up with this painting. The chaps on the cowboy on the right are one of my best efforts on this particular subject. They are made of stiff, heavy leather. Notice how the shadow of the cowboy holding the cigarette falls across them and makes an interesting pattern. Collection Pal's Cabin Restaurant, West Orange, New Jersey.

DEMONSTRATION 18
Chaps

Chaps protect cowboys from horse, saddle horn, bramble, and snake bite. This is another cowboy item that originated south of the border. The name of these partial leather trousers is from the Mexican-Spanish "chaparajos." When a cowboy dons chaps atop spurred, high-heeled boots, he cuts down his mobility on foot more than ever — somewhat like a knight in armor. Only the hockey goalie with his pads — which cowboy chaps certainly resemble — weighs in with more leather from the waist down. And the goalie is a lot more mobile in front of his cage than is a cowboy in chaps on his own front porch.

The ultimate in cowboy working gear, chaps are terribly hot in summer and cold and rigid in winter. They're heavy to drag around, along with all the other hardware the cowboy has hanging from his body during the working day. Small wonder cowboys consider sitting around motionless, stockinged feet raised high, the perfect way to cap the day.

My painting is of a rather tough trail rider I know. After a particularly hard day of work, he's pulled off his boots, loosened his chaps, and is standing around trying to decide whether it's worth the effort to change and drive into town for a few beers after supper. The final verdict isn't in yet.

The looseness of chaps and their heavy leather folds, which resist easy bending, create a lot of tonal gradation between the lightest light of the chaps, which is white, and their darkest dark, which is nearly black. This makes a very dramatic drapery effect, helping the painting tremendously. Also important to the picture are the contrast of the light vest with the chaps and the cowboy's flatfooted stance, balanced by his hands on the chap supports.

Did the bearded rider go to town that evening? I don't know. He was still padding around trying to make up his mind when I packed up my sketch box and said goodbye.

Step 1. The basic drawing of the chaps is done with a thin wash of painting medium and raw umber. In this first step I want to capture the basic drawing, the form, the proportions, and the generally loose nature of chaps. These basic aims demand a rather unstructured approach to the initial rendering. When I feel this has been accomplished, I proceed to Step 2.

Step 2. In this second step I'm only interested in very general areas—those that represent the shadowed or darker portions in the rendering. I paint these in with raw umber. They tend to blend into the wash already laid down and provide the areas I need to work with in the final two steps.

Step 3. There are many variations of colors and contrasts in this step, all of which are rendered by using flake white and a sable brush. Where I need the lightest color, I use flake white the thickest, and conversely, I apply it more thinly for the darker gradations. In this manner I'm able to create the large number of tonal gradations needed to roughly capture the heavy, deep folds in the fabric, which by its very nature does not bend easily. I outline the standing body with the hands at the waist. I now allow this step to dry completely.

Step 4. Using raw umber, I lightly glaze over the entire rendering and then allow this glaze to almost dry. Now that the glaze is sticky, I use a soft brush to blend flake white into the light areas of the folds, being careful to follow the existing brushstrokes. For the finishing touch I add the highlights in the folds using flake white with copal concentrate. Here you see the entire, completed figure.

Rifle

Raindancer. Oil on panel, 16" x 24" (40.64 x 60.96 cm). The Indian's spear is the counterpart of the cowboy's rifle. Notice how he carries it not only with sureness and ease but also with pride. This Indian is a raindancer and also a brick layer. He lives in Anadarko, Oklahoma, and is a friend of mine. This painting is done in a loose monotone style that allows the imagination to fill in some of the details. Private collection.

Rifles are used a lot more than pistols by cowboys. Most cowboy shooting is long range, and only a rifle has enough accuracy and carrying power. Getting within pistol shot of small game is difficult, and it's almost out of the question for bounding targets like mountain goats. Also, it's a lot safer, whenever possible, to stay just as far away as you can from dangerous animals like snakes or cougars.

In handling and taking care of cattle and horses miles away from the nearest veterinarian, the rifle is also a necessary tool. Sometimes cowboys have to deal instantly with animals suffering from broken legs, distemper, or other maladies for which there is no solution except immediate death. Wild, angry, unmanageable bulls or rampaging cows must often be killed on a moment's notice for their own good and human safety. Moving close to them, as would be required with a pistol, would be sheer folly. The most accurate, efficient rifle, in top working order, is appreciated by the cowboy in such situations.

Everyone who wants to learns to shoot well in the West — both white and Indian. Practicing with and taking care of a rifle are studied with an unusual intensity by most people in ranching areas. Why, I've known daughters of ranchers who, although they became stewardesses and secretaries, trained to be dead shots — veritable Annie Oakleys of the 1970s.

This picture of the cowboy holding a rifle is very much a "black and white" painting, one with plenty of contrast. The reason is that metallic parts of the gun are reduced to either extreme highlight or darkest shadow. Here is an instance where tight, careful painting is the only kind that will do. Anything else looks sloppy and unrealistic.

But this is only one aspect of the special care that must be devoted to painting a rifle. A well-constructed, draftsmanlike approach must begin with rendering proportions carefully, just as with the pistol. Later, consideration must focus on the difference in feeling and texture of metal and wood. The pronounced wood grain of the stock, with its superimposed nicks, receives most of the visual attention in this picture. Getting this right and working to vary the roundness of the rifle's surfaces requires a great deal of concentration. (The rifle shown here is taken from the complete painting that appears earlier in this book as the frontispiece.)

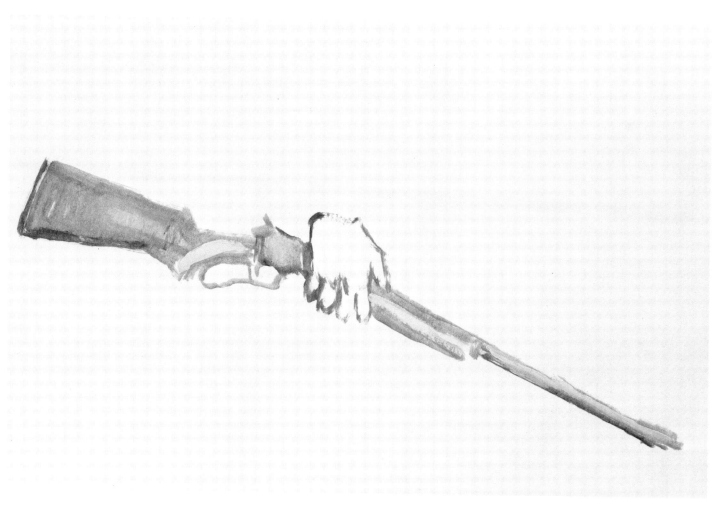

Step 1. The three colors I'm using in this step are my black, created by mixing raw umber and ultramarine blue, plain raw umber, and a combination of flake white and underpainting white. The parts of the rifle are listed from left to right: the stock, the trigger, the sideplate, the forehand, and finally the barrel. My main concern is to render their proportions and relationship accurately as well as to lay the groundwork for the wooden areas and the metal areas, which must be approached differently. Both wooden areas—the stock and the forehand—are rendered with a thin raw umber wash. I render the metal areas—which are the trigger, sideplate, and barrel—with a thin black wash. The highlights on both the wooden and the metal areas are brushed in with white. This step must now be allowed to get sticky.

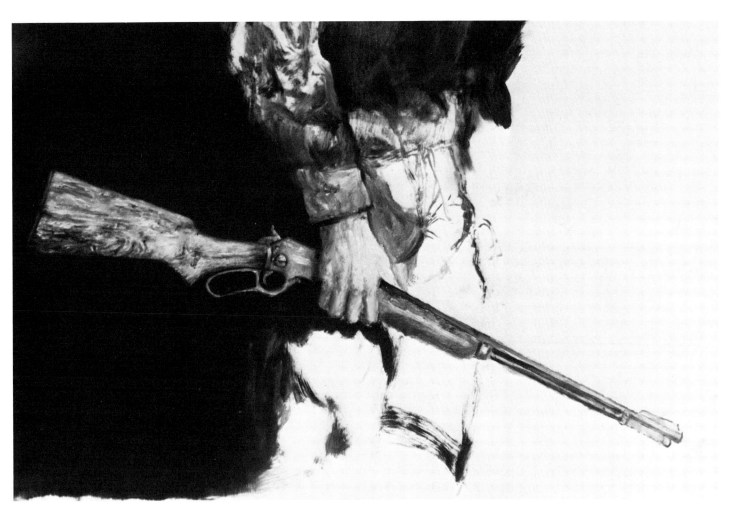

Step 2. At this point I add the figure holding the rifle. I fill in part of the background and the area surrounding a portion of the rifle in raw umber.

In this step, my primary concern is creating the wood grain of the stock. As you can see, the grain swirls at one point, and there are even nicks in the wood, which is a very common occurrence. To capture this, I scumble white into the sticky raw umber base with a small bristle brush, which creates somewhat of a grained effect. Of course, I scumble my white in the various directions the grain takes. I then change to a #2 watercolor brush and add striations of raw umber at random to further emphasize the wood grain. The nicks are simply short streaks of white and raw umber laid next to each other.

In the sideplate and trigger areas, the metal is smoothly defined by using a sable brush and working white into the sticky wash already there. A white highlight is brushed in, and details, such as the screw, are defined with black. The forehand is further detailed with raw umber and white, and a long white highlight is added. Finally, I fill in the metal barrel by working in black and white in varying degrees. This step must now be allowed to become sticky.

Step 3. All parts of the rifle are quite highly refined in this final step and I complete the figure holding the rifle and the background. Using a #2 watercolor brush, I dab, streak, and blend raw umber and white into the stock, until I'm satisfied with the effect. Notice that I darken the lower portion and add a long curving highlight near the trigger to emphasize the roundness at that point. I also place in a deep scar, which is painted in the same manner as the dents—white and raw umber are placed next to each other.

For such metal areas as the sideplate and the barrel, I just keep working in black and white until I'm satisfied, making sure the final result is quite smooth. On the barrel, I add a long, white highlight, which, when blended into the black on either side of it, creates the cylindrical appearance that is absolutely necessary.

As for the wooden forehand, I use raw umber and white so that it vaguely indicates graining. But I also add a long, pale highlight, highly blended, which serves the double purpose of indicating rounded form and a polished, smooth surface. The metal at the end of this area is almost pure white, blending into black as it rounds under the rifle.

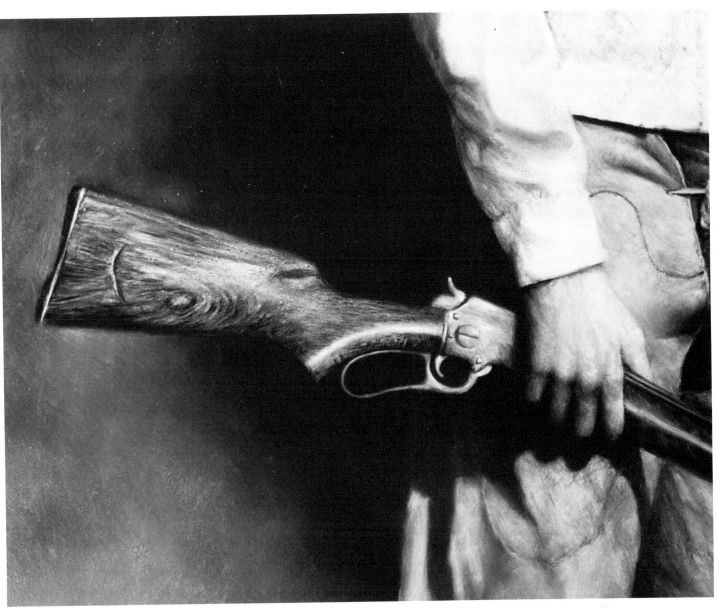

Detail. I'm including this detail of the rifle so that you can more easily see the contrast in texture and treatment between the wood and the metal. Note the hard smoothness of the metal sideplate, trigger, and hammer next to the softer, worn graininess of the wooden stock. Nicks and a large scar—the result of years of hard wear—help define the "woody" character of the stock. In both the stock and the metal parts, I've used highlights to establish the roundness of the forms and to convey their highly polished surfaces. Note too the marked difference in texture between the sharply defined highlights and shadows of the rifle's surface and the soft modeling of the hand and the clothing.

Shaking Out His Boot. Oil on panel, 8″ x 10″ (20.32 x 25.4 cm). When a West Texas cowboy puts on his boots in the morning, he should shake them out. Scorpions and spiders love to spend the night there! Notice the saddle in this picture with its rough, textured, worn leather. Always an interesting prop, the saddle can be used for background in so many ways to enhance the interest in a painting. Here it hangs unobtrusively over the hitching rail and is a very important part of the painting without really having that much to do with the main theme. Private collection.

Saddle

Saddles are the most expensive, complicated pieces of gear a cowboy deals with. His main investments are saddle and horse, so when he handles them alone or together, you can be sure it's with tender, loving care. A lot of work goes into maintaining them. Almost as much attention is given to oiling and polishing a saddle as to feeding and grooming a horse, because untended leather does not fare well against the elements. Rain, sun, heat, and sand can ruin an uncared-for saddle in a few days. That's why a cowboy treats it so preciously.

Whether the saddle is on the horse, in the tack room, on the corral fence, or by the campfire, it's likely to be foremost in the cowboy's thoughts. Saddles might be compared with major leaguers' well-worn and tended gloves. Both these leather tools take a long time to break in. Without them, their owners would ply their trades a lot less skillfully. That's why they care so deeply about them.

A saddle is a series of textures — slick leather, worn leather, tight leather, loose leather, and leather strips. Also attached are smooth and tooled metal. So my approach to painting saddles — this one is being carried by a cowboy — is to use a lot more variety than usual in my initial application of paint. This is to remind myself all through the picture not to let my attention wander from my goal of making the saddle look like the dynamic, contrasting creation it is.

Saddles cast strong shadows because they consist of broad, curved planes layered one on top of the other. In addition, these shapes are extremely interesting as abstractions. Because of its high degree of abstraction, this picture can almost be thought of as a "modern" painting. Don't ever forget, there's plenty of top-grade abstract painting in all good realism.

In developing all these saddle abstractions, textures, and contrasts, I keep values somewhat lighter than they actually are to leave myself room for the many more values that I usually incorporate. While I do this, I make sure I apply paint thickly in heavily textured areas. You might compare my approach to the careful way the leather worker goes about constructing saddles and to the manner in which the cowboy maintains them.

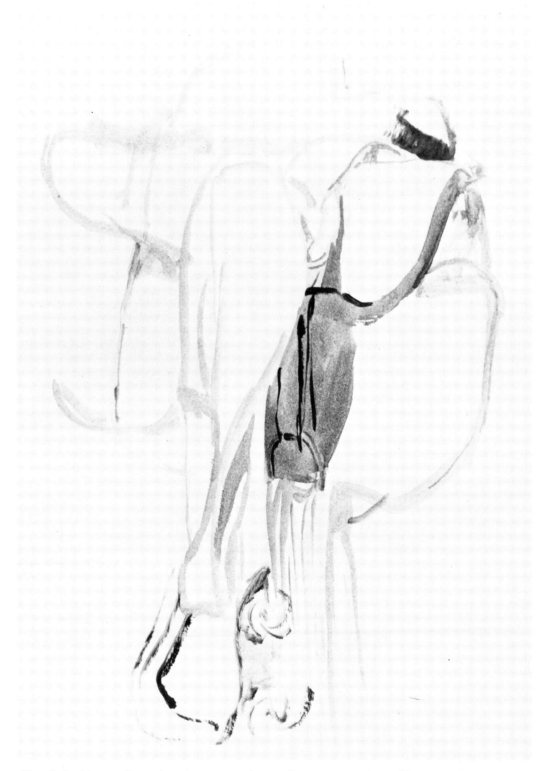

Step 1. In this step I'm only using raw umber and painting medium. My main objective in this step is to render the basic shape and proportions of the saddle accurately and to indicate the most prominent shadows. I use raw umber mixed with less painting medium in the shadow areas.

Step 2. I introduce the character who is carrying the saddle. My palette now includes white, which is a mixture of flake white and underpainting white. I have one basic aim in this step: to build up a base of thick paint for the highly textured areas. While this is my main concern, I do want to capture the values as I work. I achieve this by mixing the values with raw umber and white quite a bit lighter than they actually are, instead of using my premixed tones. As I work, I'm applying the paint very thickly and in a loose manner. It's thicker where the texture will be more pronounced and not quite so thick in the shadow areas. I let this step sit and dry completely before beginning Step 3.

Step 3. What I'm doing in this step is glazing over the entire saddle with a thin glaze of raw umber. After doing this, I take a dry bristle brush and remove the glaze in the lightest areas, which gives the impression of texture since I'm working over a base of very thickly applied paint. I create my degrees of light and dark in this manner: I remove more glaze where lighter tones are desired, and less where it will remain darker, and then add raw umber with a flat sable brush where the darkest tones appear. The background is done in raw umber. The paint should almost dry, but be slightly sticky before you go on to Step 4.

Step 4. To do the rough leather of the saddle, I take lead white mixed with copal concentrate, and using a flat sable brush, I let it glide over the top of the rough underpainting, further creating the textured effect. Highlights are particularly prominent along the edges and these I emphasize with white. I paint in the metal rings with a blending technique, using both raw umber and white. White mixed with painting medium is then tinted in, with highlights of white added as the final touch. For the darker areas, raw umber is lightly scumbled in. I blend it well in the areas where it represents forms and shadows. For the finishing touch, I complete the character who is carrying the saddle.

150

Indian Pottery

Pueblo Boy. Oil on canvas, 24" x 30" (60.96 x 76.2 cm). I found this young Pueblo boy an interesting study — not only because of his expression, but also because of his costume. The typical bandana is present, the Indian vest, and the patterned waist band. Indian patterns vary greatly and are found on clothing as well as pottery. They are readily recognizable as Indian designs and are both colorful and symmetrically designed. They are an interesting part of Indian culture wherever they are found. Private collection.

Indian pottery and ceramics are the foundation of whole Indian cultures from South America to Canada. Working with hands in earth rich in clays and colors, native Americans built out of the substance of the land jars, pots, utensils — and even homes. Artistic expression by an entire people was perhaps at no higher level than in the Aztec, Inca, and Pueblo cultures. The almost total lack of this "art spirit" in industrialized lands today is one possible reason why the populace feels so alienated.

The lovely Indian urn or vase in this demonstration was hand formed on a pottery wheel and then decorated and colored with a series of glazes and firings until its beautiful raised design was created.

This representation of the vase approximately follows the ceramic procedure. I first "sculptured" the piece by careful use of graduated shadows to impart shape and solidity. Then I added the design by painting its simple elements in a graduated manner, making sure the parts of the scheme adhered to the shadow values already established. This means each decoration was graded in value, following existing shadow strength from dark to light.

Also important to the picture is a sense of balance and attunement between the girl's body and her urn. I devoted special care to the way she holds her head and guides the pottery with her hand.

I think there's a great deal of pride and serenity in this painting — the result, no doubt, of a harmonious culture that values beauty in its members' lives.

Step 1. Raw umber and white
are the colors I use to create my
five basic tones. In this step I'm
using a sable brush and striving
to render the shape of the vase
and the manner in which it sits
on the woman's head. I use both
tones #1 and #3 to render the
shapes and shadow and to blend
the form shadow in the middle of
the vase.

Step 2. I brush in a background
of tone #2 and tone #3 thinned
with painting medium. This helps
give the vase a three-dimensional
depth and roundness, and it also
helps me correct errors in my
original drawing. Tone #2 is
placed between tones #1 and #3
and blended to help achieve a
rounded effect in the center of the
vase. To darken the shadow
areas previously denoted with
tone #3, I brush in tone #4.

Step 3. I'm adding the girl's hand
and head, which hold the vase,
and the upper part of her body.
Along the far right shadowy side
of the background by the vase, I
paint in tone #2 to represent back
lighting or reflection. This is almost always found along the
dark edge of a rounded object.
For the highlights in the vase, I
paint in tone #0. Before proceeding, I allow the paint to get sticky
overnight, or approximately eight
hours.

Step 4. (Right) The basic problem in
this step is to create the design
while maintaining the light and
dark areas needed to define the
form. Fortunately, most pottery designs are fairly simple geometric
shapes, so the problem becomes
one basically of rendering a pattern
line darker in the shadowy areas
and lighter in the lighter areas. I
use all the tones to do this. If you
bear in mind the essential aim, it's
not that difficult a task and creates
very rewarding results, as the
finished portrait shows.

DEMONSTRATION 22
Indian Dress

Indian Princess. Oil on canvas, 24" x 28" (60.96 x 71.12 cm). The Indian maiden who posed for this painting had just been chosen the princess of the tribe. She was a beautiful, slender young woman in a satin, yellow dress. The painting was done on very heavy linen, and therefore I had to build up the paint very thick. This made it a little more difficult to get the gentle, subtle fold in the material of the dress, which is better suited for a smoother surface. When painting material of this kind, I always try to get as much color into the folds and shadows without completely destroying the realism. Here, for instance, I used a subtle amount of cobalt violet in the folds of the yellow dress, along with ultramarine blue and burnt sienna. Collection Charles French.

Indian dresses are not limited to deerskin or rough hopsacking. Traditional designs created in silks and satins have been worn by Indian women since before the turn of the century. Setting off these lovely high-collared, full-sleeved costumes are beadwork necklaces, pendants, belts, and pigtail holders. The overall impression is more Oriental than is usually associated with the American Indian. But we should remember, Indians have definitely Asian origins. As most ethnic groups now recognize, peace of mind and sense of identity largely depend on keeping up folkways and traditions, like those represented by this Indian dress.

Dresses like this soft, shining one lend dignity to my subject and enhance the beauty of her black hair, bright eyes, and fine complexion. My first thought in planning the painting was to work on the dress in as smooth an oil technique as I could devise. This was so the dress would contrast sufficiently with the dabbed-in, stippled beading that ornaments the ensemble.

To achieve this smoothness, I used a watercolorlike approach in oil with a sable brush. Thinning a black mixture with plenty of painting medium did the trick for the initial satiny surface. I built upon and emphasized this surface with dark shadows created by deep folds, so characteristic of smooth, silken fabrics.

Also contributing to the sheen of the dress was a black glaze late in the painting. I flooded this over the entire torso and then wiped it from the beadwork areas. The beads in this painting are almost entirely random dabs, created mostly by suggestion, with the viewer's eye filling in the final touches. Beaded areas are thus freed of rigidity, which so easily can take over large surfaces filled with minute objects.

Pulling the picture together, and making the dress really shimmer, is the black background. It is in harmony with the garment's black accents. The completed picture is, I hope, fitting testimony to the aspirations of Indian women in the last quarter of this century.

Step 1. On my palette are raw umber and ultramarine blue, which I combine to make a black. This black is thinned with painting medium to the consistency of a watercolor wash, which is what I'll work with exclusively in this step. I'll also work with a soft sable brush. My main objective is to use this wash to block in the sleeve and the portion of the dress that is not hidden by either beads or belt. At the same time I block in the shape of the head, the hand, the beads, and the belt to help me render the proportions accurately. The prominent folds that appear mainly in the sleeve area are rendered by using the same wash, but I add much less painting medium. Before I continue, this glaze must become sticky in order to be a suitable base for Step 2.

Step 2. Flake white is now added to my palette. In this step I'll be working with the white, the black I mixed for Step 1, and a combination of this black and white that approximates tone #1. The material of the dress is light and satiny so it lends itself to a relatively smooth, simple technique. To establish a base for this, I'll use a flat, soft sable brush and apply the paint rather thinly and smoothly to avoid prominent brushstrokes. I take my tone #1 and softly brush in the light areas. I use the black to slightly darken the darker areas. In the deeply creased areas, I brush in more black. At this point I'm mainly interested in creating the soft appearance of the fabric, rather than striving to perfect the dark and light areas. To render the belt, I apply flake white in a dabbing manner, simulating the beadwork, which will be advanced later. I work in the pigtail holders with flake white in the same manner since they too are beadwork. The decorations are also dabbed in, but with tone #1. The remaining jewelry is brushed in with flake white and tone #1. I further define the head and add a hand holding feathers. This step is now allowed to dry completely.

Step 3. I begin by glazing over the entire dress with my black created in Step 1. I also use the same black for the background. Next I take a dry bristle brush and wipe the black off the beadwork areas in both the pigtail holders and the belt. The glaze remains on the dress, but I darken the very dark, shadowy areas with black and blend this into the glaze for softness. I now allow this step to sit until it reaches a nearly dry, very sticky consistency.

Step 4. The only two colors I'll be using are my previously described black and flake white. I'll also be working with a soft sable brush. To complete work on the beads, I drag white over the beads in the white areas and a combination of black and white in the darker areas. I then add the highlights on the ornaments by brushing on flake white. For the belt, I dab and drag black and white over and into the sticky surface on both the belt and its decoration. For the dress, I create my varying tones by the strength with which I apply my white, which is mixed with plenty of copal concentrate. Harder applications create darker tones as I blend them with the underpainting, and the lighter touches remain lighter. In the very dark areas of the folds, I add practically no white at all, lightly blending in black to emphasize the folds. I work in the facial features and the hand holding the feathers to complete the demonstration.

Index